MORE HEART
LESS HUSTLE

Dear Amy,
What a journey it's been.
Thank you for your support!
Jumaan
x.

More Heart, Less Hustle

Published by R&R Publishing in the United Kingdom 2025

Paperback ISBN: 978-1-0683855-0-6
eBook ISBN: 978-1-0683855-1-3

Copyright © Suman Randhawa, 2025

The moral right of Suman Randhawa to be identified as author of this work has been asserted in accordance with the Copyright, Designs and Patents Act 1988.

All rights reserved. No part of this publication may be reproduced, stored in a retrieval system, or transmitted in any form or by any means, electronic, mechanical, photocopying, recording or otherwise, without the prior permission of the copyright owners.

Publishing partnership with The Writing House, *thewritinghouse.co.uk*

Cover design by Iron Dragon Design, *irondragondesign.com*

Typesetting by The Book Typesetters, *thebooktypesetters.com*

MORE HEART
LESS HUSTLE

Generate consistent, ethical sales for
your small business

SUMAN RANDHAWA

To my late dad for always inspiring me to lead with heart.

CONTENTS

Introduction   9

SALES FOUNDATIONS

Rewrite the Story   15

A Lesson in Sales   21

The Role of Mindset   29

Reframe Your Story   39

What is Really for Sale?   47

SALES FUNDAMENTALS

Sales Fundamentals   57

The Authentic Sales Conversation   65

Confusion Kills Conversion   75

What Does the Data Tell You?   81

SALES ATTRACTION

StorySelling Through Content	97
Creating Tone Through Messaging	107
Connection to Conversion	115
The Gold is in the Repetition	125
The Fortune is in the Follow-up	133
The Value is in the Authentic Sales Voice	141

How to Stay in Touch	155
Acknowledgements	157
About the Author	159

INTRODUCTION

I know what it's like to hate sales; I used to hate them, too. That might not be the opening line you were expecting, but despite a long and successful career in sales, it wasn't always something I loved. In fact, it took me a while to find my way when starting my sales career.

When people tell me sales makes them uncomfortable, I get it. I certainly didn't plan a career in sales. I graduated into a recession, and breaking into TV or radio wasn't easy even with a media degree. A brief stint as a pirate radio DJ (illegal underground radio stations for those not old enough to know) wasn't exactly going to land me a role at the BBC either.

With few options in media, I pivoted to something more accessible but less glamorous. I came across a job advertisement for someone who was 'good with people' and 'passionate about media.' Now, that sounded like a match.

I landed a job as a classified sales assistant, selling advertising space in the back pages of a major UK tabloid. It combined everything I was good at, yet I avoided calling it 'sales' for those first few years. Truth be told, I was a little embarrassed as it wasn't as glamorous as the 'broadcaster' label I had been after.

I quickly realised sales was essential to the success of any business because without it, there was no business. I enjoyed talking to people and helping them solve problems, and I learned that listening to the answers brought in results. What I also recognised was that I wasn't motivated by the aggressive, numbers-driven environment of tabloid sales departments. Money was important to me, but it wasn't my top priority.

What truly motivated me was helping people. And that has been enough to build a successful career in sales and my business. It is also why I've continued to support others with their sales for over three decades. I love what sales allows me to do, which is to help others achieve their goals.

Early in my career, I recognised that sales reflect the energy that handles them, and I didn't have to sell like everyone else. How I felt about being sold to was a reflection of me, just as much as it was about the person selling. When I saw sales as collaborative rather than manipulative and transformational instead of transactional, things shifted for me. I led teams, managed large accounts, generated millions in sales and helped others do the same, all with more heart and less hustle.

That's why I've written this book. I see a gap for those who

INTRODUCTION

need to get the sales fundamentals right, but don't want to adopt tactics that make them feel uncomfortable, and sleazy. Many solopreneurs, coaches, and creatives – however you identify – don't relate to messaging that is about driving high volumes of leads and fast-closing tactics with acronyms that even I don't recognise half the time. If you're unsure about how to integrate sales into your business or feel disconnected from it, this book is for you.

Sales, with more heart and less hustle, is about a genuine, human approach to matching your solution with the people it can help. I'll introduce strategies that enable you to sell more authentically through connecting with clients, understanding their needs, and building relationships that lead to sales without feeling pushy.

This is for small business owners. It's for you if you find sales uncomfortable or feel you need to 'get good at it' but can't quite embrace it. It's for you if you don't resonate with the masculine, 'bro marketing' energy in sales. You know your work matters and makes a difference, but fear of selling holds you back. Bro marketers may tell you to 'do, do, do,' and while some of what they say is true – certainly without sales, there's no business – there's a way to do it differently.

You're here because you want to believe it can feel easier. You're ready for the next level in your business, and the title of this book intrigued you. Can you really sell with more heart and less hustle? Yes, you can. It's entirely possible to build a business this way, and I'm going to show you how.

The good news? A heart-led approach to sales is not only possible but effective. It puts you at the centre, and it's all about genuine human connection. Whether you're just starting or further along but want to revisit the foundations, there will be something in these pages to help you. It's not a step-by-step template but a guide to reframe your relationship with sales and remove any mental blocks stopping you from enjoying the process. Think of this as the foundation upon which coaching will build. Whether you read this book in one go or dip in and out of sections, I want it to be your go-to resource as you grow your business.

People often ask if I teach sales, I don't. Instead, I help you rethink how sales fit into your business. Let's begin with understanding your current mindset and reframe it to help you grow your business with more heart and less hustle.

PART 1

SALES FOUNDATIONS

CHAPTER 1

REWRITE THE STORY

How often do you find yourself asking 'how'?

- **How do I build a sustainable business?**
- **How do I attract my dream clients?**
- **How do I *sell* to them?**

The 'how' is super important, but the 'why' is the linchpin. Without your why, the how won't work.

In the Autumn of 2023, I announced that I had the biggest speaking gig of my career to date at one of Europe's largest small business sales and marketing conferences, Atomicon. I'd been in business less than eighteen months, yet I would be presenting alongside luminaries from the world of sales and marketing, international entrepreneurs and well-known TV personalities.

There was so much love and support when I made this announcement, and a lot of messages from women asking me, 'How? How did I make it happen?'

The answer lies in two things and these are both crucial in understanding sales.

Firstly, sales are a transaction. But that transaction isn't just about money; it's about what you offer in exchange for what you receive. For example, I am sharing my expertise and point of view in exchange for you picking up and reading this book. The 'transaction' of my knowledge for your time takes place.

Part of this transaction stems from your why. My why for the speaking gig was understanding the value I added as a female sales mentor in a space where not enough women take up space. A quick search of the term 'sales' on social media platforms like Instagram and TikTok will show you the most popular sales videos with people shouting, wearing a headset, using a flip chart, sweating, or sometimes all four.

In my pitch to be a speaker, I was able to get clear on the value I would add (so it wasn't just about why I wanted the spot). I was able to communicate my mission to show more female entrepreneurs the way with sales. But not just women. When I did go on to speak at the event, the room was packed, standing room only, despite me being relatively unknown at that time. Men, women, younger and older entrepreneurs were all interested in learning about how good people can make great sales. The writing of this book had taken a little hiatus back then, but seeing everyone in that room and the response to the talk afterwards confirmed everything I needed to know. People wanted to know how to sell in a more heart-led way.

You can sell more by selling less. Which I like to call 'more heart, less hustle'. There is such a thing as overselling. And this imbalance comes from the focus being on the selling rather than the serving. It's a subtle but essential difference.

When you serve, you come from a place of seeking to understand what someone needs versus how you can best help. The serve part of the equation comes from genuinely wanting to establish what is best for your dream client at that moment. The ultimate goal is not, you may be surprised to hear, to make a sale. It is to identify a match. And the higher the value of what you sell, the more this becomes key.

I have sold everything from classified space in the back of a newspaper, a multi-million-pound diamond (as part of a sales team), through to my mentoring services to small business owners. One thing remained the same. At the heart of every great sale was understanding the needs of the individual buying. Even when I worked in markets where my fees were not the cheapest, I could grow my business and maintain client loyalty through the power of relationship building.

What more heart and less hustle does not mean is

avoiding difficult conversations. Even in coaching and mentoring, helping someone identify the support they need to move forward can involve uncomfortable conversations. But the key difference is that your role in this 'transaction' is to help them seek clarity about those next steps, with or without you. The sales part of the conversation is to demonstrate how you can best help. This may include how your support will help them get there quicker, perhaps saving time, offering accountability, support to pivot, etc. Or simply offering greater certainty of the result versus doing it on their own.

Throughout my sales career, I am most comfortable and have seen the most success with a more heart-led, intuitive style of selling. One where the client is at the centre of the conversation.

The second thing I did to help secure my coveted speaking gig (and this one might throw you, so prepare yourself) was… ask for it. The second fundamental part of understanding sales is that when the fit feels right, you get to ask for or invite the sale, and there will be more on this later. You can't be rejected because it is not you who is for sale. The transaction is between the service you offer and what is received in return.

These two parts are how I landed my biggest speaking gig. I tapped into my why and it formed part of what I offered in the transaction. I then made a choice, and this is where it starts. I simply put myself forward with a people-centric, heart-led approach to sales I knew small business owners needed to learn more about.

I challenge you to look at sales differently and ask yourself if the discomfort of not reaching more people through the work you do is greater than the discomfort of selling, as this is your sales story. Ask yourself how you would feel if you invited more of the right people to a conversation with you versus if you did not reach out to more people who you could help. Which feeling is stronger for you – avoiding speaking to them or the desire to change lives with your work?

CHAPTER 2

A LESSON IN SALES

How you feel when being sold to usually says a lot about your thoughts around selling. This is why it is important to reflect on where your sales blueprint, your sales story, came from.

If you are the core target audience of this book (female business owners aged 40+) you'll have grown up in the 1970s or 1980s. And if you are not in that exact target audience, it is proof that niching will not exclude other people from being interested in learning about your work. But more on that later. If you grew up in those decades, you'll most likely remember a door-to-door sales approach, possibly even double-glazing salesmen. They would stay for hours and insisted on speaking to both 'Mum and Dad'. You might even recall a visit from the Encyclopaedia Britannica salesman.

It was a time of no mobiles or the internet, which limited intel and data, and men still dominated sales. The impactful women we did see were rocking shoulder pads, bouffant hair, and big ball energy.

This was a far cry from the society we see today. Data and technology have led to a more customer-centric approach, trust plays a big part in sales and depending on which piece of research you read, the average person sees a message thirty plus times before they buy. This number is fast rising and was even updated during the writing of this book. And 'seeing' a message today can be done through a plethora of ways, from social media, TV, outdoor advertising, email to word of mouth.

As a society, we are also far more touchy-feely than the sales approach you may have grown up with. The harder sales approach of the 1980s not only put many people off from entering a career in sales but also lingered in our psyche when approaching sales later in our lives.

Fast forward to the current decade, you launch your own business, and you may see messaging from 'bro marketers' all over your social media feed telling you to sell with a more aggressive approach. Depending on which algorithm you have been served, you might see flashy cars, hyped-up videos and more persuasion than attraction as a sales approach. Which is why you might be left feeling misaligned. This was not the energy with which you launched your business and possibly walked away from a corporate career.

These 'bro marketers' have been around as long as the

internet and much of their sales tactics are around scarcity, which creates pressure for the potential buyer. Many are the next generation of used cars and double-glazing salesman. And whilst I do teach and believe in a reason for 'why now', it's not to create false alarm. It's to help potential dream clients cut through the noise and decide why now is the time.

If the language of sales back then was 'buy now', the current language gets to be 'buy when'. This means identifying who is ready to step forward now. You are helping your dream clients by making it easier for them to recognise themselves in your content. This is on your website, social media posts and in your conversations. Embracing the 'more heart, less hustle' style of sales I teach helps you take steps away from unethical tactics.

Even for the ambitious, there is an increasing awareness of the need for work-life balance. Mental fitness is a priority, alongside how neurological diversity may impact the way you work. These shifts, alongside a world that feels smaller, means we are more connected and more aligned with what is going on in the world socially and politically. With this awareness comes a greater sense of responsibility, which lends itself to a more aligned way of selling.

The flip side is that with more information, speed and technology many feel they are doing more, with less time than ever. Technology adds to immediacy and speed and has also changed the need for transparency. Customer reviews and competitive pricing are quickly accessible at the touch of a button, which means there is far greater transparency for the person buying.

For us to shift into this new approach to sales we firstly have to reconcile how we have always viewed selling. This begins by looking back at our childhood.

- When did you see examples of sales?
- What was the industry?
- What do you remember about the approach?
- What was the outcome?

Answering these questions might help you to uncover your first blueprint of sales. Look at what you have written and consider how this may have impacted you subsequently.

My extensive career in sales started in the mid-1990s, before launching my own business as a sales mentor in 2021. In one of my first sales roles working for a tabloid newspaper in telesales, I was selling classified spots at the back of the newspaper. We were measured on how many calls we made, and how quickly we picked up the phone. I also remember the dreaded Monday morning meeting where one of the managers would go through the competitor newspapers and you were asked to explain any advertising that you were not carrying. It was not the calmest way to start my week! It was pretty scarring, but as I moved into sales in magazines, I saw

A LESSON IN SALES

a softer approach and noticed two key areas that I loved:

1. Data – which helped to understand behaviours and habits
2. Partnerships – which are relationships with aligned brands that widen your reach

I appreciated this more integrative form of selling, where what was sold was not only more relevant to the reader but more seamlessly integrated into the magazine editorial. For the first time in my career, I saw sales as a more consultative, collaborative storytelling approach, and fell in love with what I did.

I had always thought sales was the less sexy sister of marketing. But this changed as I saw how much value can be added to a consumer when a partnership feels relevant and targeted. And I saw what great sales does for the customer. We had far more access to insight, surveys and tools that helped our team really understand who we were serving and what they thought and felt. This became my first foray into a more heart-led sales approach.

When you have worked in sales for as long as me, you have seen the highs of the commission-heavy heydays, the lows or busts and recessions, and the in-between. As magazine sales fell in the noughties due to the increase of social media, websites, blogs, and digital and cable TV channels vying for audience attention, advertisers wanted to decrease what they were paying based on falling audience numbers. As a sales team, our negotiations with the advertisers centred around demonstrating how valuable, loyal and engaged our readers were, and the bigger impact of targeting them and minimising wastage, rather than just focusing on how many magazines we were selling. We believed this made the audience even more valuable.

Why am I telling you all of this?

Because it became relevant in helping me identify not only where I felt most comfortable in sales, but where I became the most creative in finding a solution when the buyers wanted to pay less. It becomes important to understanding the value your audience adds. The greater your understanding of your audience, the greater the connection between you and the buyer. I went on to work in many different markets, and all of this taught me the value of getting super clear on who your potential end customer is and what outcome they want.

The vast majority of people make the decision to buy based on emotions. This is what I mean when I say throughout this book, sell the transformation or the end result to your clients, which is often an emotion. What we aren't selling is the transportation, such as how many modules are in your course.

In one of my early sales interviews, I recall being asked to sell a pen. A quick YouTube search will show you similar examples, I am sure. Whilst it sounds a bit nineties (it was) the key here is they weren't looking for the description of the pen but what the pen would allow the person buying it to do.

This book recognises that you most likely picked it up because you want to get better at sales, or if you do 'dislike' sales you are here because you want to change that. You will hear many people tell you to focus on what you are good at, but for the first few years of your entrepreneurial journey, it is not always possible to outsource everything you struggle with. So, what happens when you don't like the sales, find it difficult, and in turn don't see the results?

It gets to feel different if you reframe how you feel about selling and consider what is holding you back first rather than just finding a way to make you do it.

Now that you have reflected on your early sales blueprint and my own, can you see how different it could look? What would it feel like if almost all of your sales conversations turned into a yes? And hearing a 'no' didn't unsettle your confidence in yourself and your services. If you didn't feel you had to persuade anyone and you didn't see a no as a rejection?

Makes you think, doesn't it?

To continue this journey, let's take a look at the mindset that helps support greater sales in your business.

CHAPTER 3

THE ROLE OF MINDSET

If you picked up this book to learn how you can sell more, you picked up the wrong book.

Now before you shut the book in disgust, hear me out.

Is selling uncomfortable simply because you don't see the results and struggle with a feeling of rejection? As I have already shared, they can't reject you – because you are not what's for sale. This powerful reframe can help you separate what is for sale, the transformation, from you. Yes, you may be the person who delivers it, but what your potential client is buying is the result or at least some degree of certainty of the result.

Selling may feel particularly uncomfortable when you consider your history with 'sales' and that this memory may feel out of alignment with industries where you change people's lives, but therein lies my point. If you don't let people know how you can help and make it easier for them to get your help, you may feel stuck when progressing with sales. And any sales tools you access or 'learn' will be ineffective if you still have a difficult relationship with how you view sales.

Simon Sinek is a renowned leadership expert, speaker, and author, best known for his groundbreaking work on the importance of purpose-driven leadership. His TED Talk, 'How Great Leaders Inspire Action,' introduced the powerful idea of starting with why, which is understanding the deeper purpose behind what we do. I'm going to ask you to consider the same for your business, so you see the worth in your part of the transaction:

- Why do you do what you do?
- Can you recall the moment you knew?
- Why did you decide this was important to you?
- What's your bigger goal for the world through the work that you do?
- Why is this important to you?

Once you are reminded of your why, consider what happens when or if you don't get to reach more of the people whose lives you can change through your work. It doesn't feel quite like selling now, does it?

Another equally powerful mindset reframe that will help get the results you want is asking for a sale more than once.

THE ROLE OF MINDSET

As I shared in the last chapter, research shows that on average people need to see/hear a message thirty plus times (and rising) before they buy for the first time. Most people have a million other things going on in their lives, so buying your product or service may not be top of their mind. This is why it is helpful to repeat the same message more than once. This means mentioning the solution you offer for the problem your dream client faces, not just once and wondering why no one steps forward. It's not necessarily about you or your offer.

By making the offer more than once, you are making it easier for someone to recognise themselves in your description of the symptoms of the problems they face and understand why and how you can help. Repeating this message in different ways, for example, through SEO content, social media, emails or even direct mail (if you are GDPR compliant), is about making it easier for people to step forward and see the message. When your intention for selling comes from an authentic place, your delivery will be more authentic. Alongside reminding yourself that you are serving, it can help reposition sales when you feel uncomfortable. The reason we are looking at thirty plus touchpoints is because we are inundated with information, so messages have to work even harder to be seen.

What you are looking for is to attract, not persuade. This is the opposite of the double glazing and bro marketeer's approach. You are supporting this potential client with the belief that now is the time, they are ready to change, and this is the investment they want to make. Layered on top are the tools to do this. These tools are your online courses, workbooks, an app or in-person masterclass. While most people do make the decision to buy based on emotion, they justify it based on logic.

Much like it starts with the mindset of your clients towards the work you do, it starts there for you too. If you believe that:

- Selling is embarrassing (or annoying)
- Selling is not a daily part of your business
- Selling is not 'you'

Then you are going to struggle. I want you to reframe sales and recognise the value of understanding how what you offer transforms your dream clients' lives – and how valuable that transformation is. This leads to believing in the value of you. If your value remains, sales do not detract or add to that.

What you are selling your dream clients needs to speak to specific examples of how a problem shows up in their life. For example, if you were a health coach, you may be speaking to potential clients who say they want to 'lose weight' and need the motivation to start running. But your expertise might tell you they need something else. As the expert, you know they really need to focus on their why and diet first, for example.

For your messaging to really resonate with your audience, we need to show the reality of not having this outcome for your dream client in their daily life. For example, if they are a mum of young children, do they struggle to keep up with an energetic toddler? They know it's not a great situation, yet they feel too tired to go to the gym after a hectic morning getting their children ready for nursery. Speak to such examples in your messaging; this is where they will recognise themselves and see how you can help them despite the challenges they face.

If what puts you off sales is that it is about making money, I invite you to see things differently. A client once told me she was worried she would annoy her audience on social media if she repeatedly mentioned how someone could buy. My response was that if someone isn't choosing to be connected on social media to either support, be inspired or buy – what are they doing there? I also firmly believe that as adults if your content or emails no longer feel relevant, they can choose to unfollow.

When it comes to competitors in your field, you can also choose who inspires you or who you don't want to watch. Whichever route you take, don't let it distract you from your mission to help more people whose lives you can change through your work. What would more sales in your business allow you to do? How could you reinvest this money? What would it allow you to do philanthropically? Considering these questions, how do you feel about asking for the sale, supporting someone and receiving money into your account in exchange for the transformation you can offer?

Historically, sales were about hitting targets. But times have changed and you get to change with them. The mindset shift with sales is about understanding why sales matter and how they allow you to change the lives of those you support.

TASK 1: PAIN POINTS

Throughout the book, I have shared short tasks to enable you to implement your understanding of the chapters and apply them to your business and clients.

As we have seen, it always starts with the foundations. Even if you think you know the answers, I invite you to set aside some time to check if your current clients and audience are who you expect them to be. Because as you grow and evolve, the likelihood is so will your dream clients.

Your first task is to consider your dream client and five specific key problems or daily challenges they face as a result of not having the support they need. The extent of the problem may not be the same in every industry, so if the term 'problem' does not feel applicable to your service, consider what would cause them to be looking for a solution.

THE ROLE OF MINDSET

Now list these as five points, with each one consisting of a detailed sentence that explains the situation. If you need prompts to help with this, consider the answers to these questions:

- What does your dream client believe to be true?
- Why does your dream client believe this problem or pain point still exists?
- What does your dream client think is the solution?
- What is your dream client aspiring to?

Drill down with each question so you get to the specificity of the answer. Here is an example of a career coach to help you.

Starting Point:
The career coach helps dream clients find a job.

Why is this?
Because their dream client feels dissatisfied.

Why is she dissatisfied?
She is not enjoying her role.

Why is she not enjoying her role?
Because she feels like she is in the wrong job.

How does that impact her?
She faces dread every Sunday, impacting her weekends and time with family.

So, the last point, as we drilled down, would be your first specific example of what that problem looks like for your dream client. Now, come up with your examples by doing the same exercise.

5 Key Pain Points of your dream client
e.g. She no longer wants to face the dread of Sunday nights as she anticipates getting back to work

1. _____

_____

2. _____

_____

3. _____

_____

THE ROLE OF MINDSET

4. _____

_____

5. _____

_____

Next, consider the main solutions you offer. Again, consider five points, and each should be a complete sentence. An example of what this might look like for a career coach is: 'A Strength Finder. I use positive psychology to help you better understand your natural talents and increasing your opportunities at work.'

Now, identify yours.

1. _____

_____

2. _____

_____

3. _____

_____

4. _____

_____

5. _____

_____

Once you have reviewed the two lists, consider if what you offer (the transformation) matches what your dream client is looking for. If it's not, then you have a mismatch and may need to reassess your messaging – it's as important to be clear who you are able to support as well as those that wouldn't be a match.

CHAPTER 4

REFRAME YOUR STORY

Without sales, there is no business. Let that sink in. Unless you can drive sales, you will not have a business.

What I am not saying is that you only need sales to succeed in business. There are many important elements of your business: branding, networking, social media content, cash flow, collaborations, bookkeeping and accounting, organic and paid-for marketing, design and copywriting. The list goes on. And yet sales (and cash flow) are the consistents that will keep your business flowing.

For those of you who chose to work for yourself to achieve more balance, you'll know for the first few years balance is a myth. You're pulled in every direction and bombarded with advice on what you should prioritise. What should you be focusing on in your business first? Depending on who you speak to, you will get a different answer.

However, one thread that runs through all you have 'to do' is the need to understand who your audience is, attract them (through your preferred or most effective method), build their trust, and connect and nurture them. The final part is your ability to turn conversations and calls into clients, which at times might feel as difficult as turning water into wine.

Which part of the process outlined above would you have described as sales? The most common response is likely to be the final part, the sales conversation. Yet sales are in everything you do. Your website is selling how you want to be seen (the first impression), the font you use might show whether you have a contemporary or more traditional way of thinking, the colours of your branding may be warm, scientific or show you are an out-of-the-box thinker, and the words you write on your social media posts will call people in who feel you are speaking to them. These are a few examples, and they are all part of sales. I discovered early in my career that to be great at sales, the key elements are:

- To get clear on your story (how you help your dream client and why you are the best person to help).

- To understand how to speak to your dream clients (which is done best when you understand your dream clients' needs and what you can do for them).

- To make it easy for them to recognise themselves in your story, (as if you were speaking directly to them).

I call these the attract, connect and convert stages of sales. The reason I break it down in this way is to demonstrate how sales is a thread running through the entire journey of your business. Getting great at sales isn't just about learning how to sell. It is also about understanding why they are important to your business, understanding how they tap into your 'why' for launching your business and, done well, allows you to attract more of the right people into your world and impact more people through the work that you do. Furthermore, before you sell, you must nurture. Nurturing is building connection, trust and community. All these elements are very much part of sales.

The purpose of this chapter, now you have considered your history with sales, is to show you how to love the selling part of your business because of what it allows you to do. It's not just about making money, that's a beautiful by-product of what you do, it's about transforming lives. That's powerful stuff, which won't happen without exchanging the solution you offered for the problem solved.

Sales allows you to make money, the connotations around the making of money may be deep-seated in your mind and history as sleazy, greedy, out of reach or lacking in your life. And that thinking can also subconsciously stop you from inviting the sale.

But what if you were to look at it differently? You'll be familiar with the saying 'You can't pour from an empty cup'. You also can't pay from an empty business. Therefore, consider what you can do from a business that has enough income from sales to provide paid employment for those it can support, in turn helping you grow your business and potentially allowing you more time to volunteer, donate, support an individual or organisation, and so on. If any of those appeal to you, alongside being able to afford to provide for yourself and your loved ones, then it's yet another reason why you would benefit from reframing your sales story.

When I look back at my very first job in sales that I took on back in the mid-1990s, I can still remember the outfit I wore to my interview. I'd had to buy my power suit using store credit from a premium high street store, but that investment gave me the freedom of a salary that allowed me to do more things in life. In return, the transaction was that I offered my skill set so that potential advertisers (dream clients at that time) could reach more of the people they wanted to speak to through the newspaper I worked for.

All these years later, the money I earn is for more meaningful reasons. But it also allows me to live my chosen lifestyle and make my desired impact in the world. What would more money in your business allow you to do? And what will reaching and helping more people, allow them to do? The benefits of sales are limitless. Your answer will help you reframe your sales story.

Now consider how you have felt about tasks in your business and identify your personal sales pressure points. What are you saying in your content and messaging (website, blogs, social media posts) – does this feel natural, and does it sound like you? There are, of course, templates, styles and methods that lend themselves to creating content with greater ease in these places.

But templates aside, what is the story you are telling your dream clients? Are they being taken on a journey to connect with you, and is it clear what is unique about how you can help? The most unique part of your business is most likely you. As I have mentioned, research tells us that most people will make their decision to buy based on an emotional connection (justified by logic) rather than for practical reasons. This is why learning about what drives an emotional response is essential for any healthy business.

You, therefore, need to connect with your dream clients at a deeper level. They need to feel something when they read your content and to recognise themselves in it. And for that to happen, you must speak to them in a way that resonates, which means understanding them.

Below is an exercise I encourage you to do at least once a quarter. It is quite common that you built your business around an issue or problem that you once faced, and it is, therefore, not unusual to make assumptions. This is why I encourage quarterly audits as you grow and evolve, because so will your audience, and the challenges you support clients with now may not be the same as they faced a year ago. Ask yourself:

- When was the last time you spoke to your dream clients to understand the symptoms of their main pain points?
- How does this show up in daily life or business for them?
- When did you last sense check that against the services you offer?
- How clear are you about how a potential client is feeling before working with you versus the transformation after they work with you?

This book is written predominantly with female entrepreneurs in mind who offer their services online and work in fields that encompass some form of transformation for their dream clients. I often see that what holds someone back is not their sales call structure (although that is important), it is a lack of belief in their ability to sell or a belief that 'doing sales' is uncomfortable for them and their potential clients. Your energy leads any situation, before anything you say or sell. And that translates both in person and through your messaging.

As I have shared in this chapter, for sales to be most effective, understand its purpose in your business, be prepared to let go of the negative connotations and embrace how sales don't just transform your life but, most importantly, the lives of people you can help.

Therefore, your job is not to convert every sales call or you will be selling to people who aren't ready or aren't your dream clients. It's to help your dream clients identify where they want to be, where they currently are and show them what is keeping them stuck. With that information, they can then decide if they want the support to get there, and if they are a match for what you offer.

As this book was written predominantly with service-based online businesses in mind, you might wonder whether this advice also applies to product-based small businesses. The answer is yes. If you or a member of your team are selling to an individual, as almost all of you will be in product-based businesses, there is a reason your potential client is going to choose you over a competitor. And the higher the investment to buy your product or service and the bigger the transformation, the more there is to consider. So, whether you are selling window shutters or anxiety coaching, the price points may be similar or not, but the considerations are the same.

Does your product or service understand your audience's needs? Does your dream client feel a greater degree of certainty that working with you will get them closer to their goals than not? And with both examples, it's not the structure of the programme or the style of blinds that you are selling, it is the impact they will have on your dream client. How will it make them feel about themselves or, as in the example of the blinds, their homes?

A great approach to sales isn't about a product or service. It is about how it takes your client from point A, where they are, to point B, where they want to be. This impact is the transformation.

At the heart of how to become skilled in sales, is understanding what is for sale. Which is where we'll go next.

CHAPTER 5

WHAT IS REALLY FOR SALE?

Now we have spent some time getting clear on what sales is and what happens when you start to think about sales differently, we can reflect on how to separate yourself from any potential feeling of rejection if your sales are not on track. Often hidden behind the objection of 'I don't have the time right now' or 'I don't have the money' is fear. Fear that they cannot make it work or a belief that it will not work for them.

To counteract this, it's your job to get super clear on what you sell. Let me explain with my own example. In 2023, my biggest coaching investment was made based on the coach's reputation. I saw it as my job to convince the coach why they should take me on. I did not ask for details about their programme because I was already convinced this coach was the best one to help me reach my goals.

That's because I bought into the possibilities of the transformation I desired. It was a commitment to their stellar reputation and the belief they could guide me to my goals. The details became secondary because I was already sold on the transformative possibilities I had imagined. In essence, it's not just a sale; it's an investment in the journey towards the next destination.

Consider how you explain what you do and how you help someone achieve their goal. How is this currently described on your website or in your content? Now, I'd like you to recall how you last introduced yourself at an event or dinner party with people you don't know. That moment when you are sitting next to a stranger, and they most likely have a person on either side of them, and they ask you what you do. The cluster of sentences you share will either create interest, drive an association or lead them to quickly turn to the person sitting on their other side. Those key sentences should roll off the tongue when anyone recalls who you help, what you help them do and how you do it.

I was recently at a networking event and the host took us around the room as each person introduced themselves. Some 'brief introductions' went on for ten minutes, and I noticed some of the audience started talking as their attention was lost. One of the women in the room was a therapist who ran retreats, and she was there with her very loyal friend whose life had been turned around by one of those retreats.

The therapist gave a brief introduction, which was done in seconds. Her friend then turned to the room and told everyone that her friend was underselling her retreats and how her life had been truly changed as a result of attending. She described how life felt before and how life was after. The audience was captivated, and even days later, I remembered little about anyone else's introductions in the room apart from a clear memory of the story her friend shared. That's the power of storytelling and an emotional connection. Stop playing yourself down for fear of sounding big-headed or ruffling feathers. It should be clear who you are for (and who you are not for).

We have faced a global pandemic, global recession and wars. There is a belief by some that people are not spending on higher ticket items. This is not what I see, and in the luxury personal goods market, studies continue to show that spending is increasing. They are just more considered with purchases, which is why trust, reputation and image are so important. This is even more crucial within the coaching industry, where price points may seem higher, so people want to be sure of the individual they buy from. They have to believe or be shown what happens if they stay where they are versus if they were to get support to achieve their chosen result.

Let's circle back to the beginning of the chapter and what you are selling, which is not you. With sales, your focus is not on selling yourself; rather, it's showcasing the journey. Your clients should recognise where they are now, and you get to show them why what they have done before has not worked and why you have their solution. As I have shared in earlier chapters, it is important to ask your dream clients regularly where they are and how they feel.

Some of the most effective ways to do this include through your social media content (using polls to ask questions) and considering the comments on not only your content but also underneath the content of other notable people in your industry. It is important to remember that with this method of seeking feedback, be sure the information shared is from someone who would be your dream client.

The second method to gather the most effective understanding of what your dream clients are thinking or feeling is through qualifying conversations through direct messaging (DMs). These are open questions that help you understand further why someone commented or engaged with one of your posts or voted in a poll. You are identifying what it was about your content that resonated with them most. I call these qualifying questions, which, when shared at the right time and in the right way, allow you to identify whether this person is a dream client and, if so, what they are thinking, feeling right now. A useful question to ask is what it was that resonated with them and why. But be aware you might just be the tenth person who asked that question that day. So, consider how else you might say this.

The third and most effective method is to listen to what your potential clients say on sales calls. Regardless of whether they are ready to work with you now or not, an effective sales conversation is designed to help your potential clients get clearer on where they are, where they want to be, what they believe holds them back, and how committed they are to taking action. Your role in an effective sales call is to share what you see as the real reason holding them back and what they need to move forward. Not the 'how', because that's what happens when they work with you.

The information you gather about what your dream clients think they want is balanced by what you, as the expert, know they need. It's about listening to potential clients but also using your skills to help identify what is keeping them stuck or, conversely, moves them forward.

In the next part, we will consider the fundamentals that you'll most commonly associate with selling, and that starts with the skills you'll need to have great sales calls and conversations.

TASK 2: THE TRANSFORMATION

Now we have considered the origins of your sales story, what you do and the importance of it, here is a short exercise to help you understand why what you do and offer is so valuable. Remember that what we are considering here is the transformation you are offering as that is what people will connect with, not the transportation.

Based on what you have read in this section and your reflections, what is it that makes what you do so valuable? Think about the highest-priced offer you have, which should be relative to the deepest transformation you offer, but not necessarily reflective of the time spent to achieve the result.

Pricing should not be relative to time in many online coaching businesses, and this approach is taken outside the coaching world, too. Is the result of driving lessons or studying for your college grade qualifications any less because it is done as an intensive? Another example is why brides (and grooms) are charged more 'just because' it's a wedding when they buy flowers, have makeup done, and hire a car, etc. Is it unfair, inflated pricing? Or is it pricing that is reflective of the importance of that task to the individual and the impact of it not going to plan?

A quick Google search of the question of why brides are charged more may tell you it is due to the bespoke nature of the service. That's part of the reason, but the real significance is due to the importance and associated risks of it going wrong. Now, apply this same thinking to how you would price an intensive day with you versus someone who meets with you twice a month for three months. Which would you believe should be priced higher? Is the consideration of the

WHAT IS REALLY FOR SALE?

period, the amount of time it takes to get to the result or the intensity of the experience relative to the promise made? To help you do this, answer the following prompts:

Consider the following:

- What evidence do you have about the extent of the problem for your dream clients?
- What is the promised result for your dream clients?
- What makes it so valuable to your dream clients?
- What makes your offer, and how you do it, so unique?

_____

_____

_____

_____

_____

_____

_____

SALES FOUNDATIONS

_____

_____

_____

_____

_____

_____

_____

_____

_____

_____

This should be done regularly, rather than as a one-off exercise.

PART 2

SALES FUNDAMENTALS

CHAPTER 6

SALES FUNDAMENTALS

The fundamentals for great sales is not the 'gift of the gab' as you may commonly believe. To be great in sales, you don't just need to be great at closing. You need to be great at listening.

When I started in sales, we had hours of training and stood in front of a board learning various acronyms to help us 'get great at sales'. Then you'd flick through your Rolodex, pick up the phone, ask to speak to the decision maker, go through a script and, if you were any good, close a few sales.

We have moved a long way since those days, aided by changes in technology, transparency and the way we live our lives. You are not selling people a course or a programme; you are sharing a vision of how life can feel after their work with you. They are buying the belief that you are the person who will help them get there.

It goes without saying that ethics should be the heart of

everything you do in your business. This isn't Fyre Festival. You have to be equipped to support as you have promised. The role of sales comes after this.

But whilst this book isn't about teaching you modern-day acronyms, you still need to understand the sales process. Even though this process isn't always entirely linear, having a greater understanding of what the route from point A (before they work with you) to point B (after they work with you) looks like, will help.

As I have shared, the number one skill needed by all great salespeople is to listen. And by listening, I mean really understanding what your client is saying. In a world where you are running your business online, it's more important than ever to listen to what people want to achieve or no longer want in their lives. We have already identified that what differentiates you from another business is most likely going to be you, and that is where the element of differentiation in a crowded market will come in.

The adage of people buying people is important, but it's not solely what someone is buying. It is that they are more likely to achieve their goal with you than without you. If you are looking for clients (people who work with you more than once) versus customers (people who work with you once and the process feels much more transactional), then relationships are going to be key. And you can't build relationships without listening to what the other person has to say.

We are in an era where one of the most important factors for consumers is personalisation, and this comes from tailoring your offer to the individual. Wardrobes are curated, goods are crafted, and coaching is bespoke. This particularly applies if what you offer is a premium service with higher pricing (also known as high ticket), the expectation from most clients is they are going to get something shaped to what they need. The higher the touch points (the closer the contact with you), the higher the ticket price and the more bespoke the solution needs to be. What you are listening for is:

- What does your dream client want to achieve?
- What do they believe is holding them back?
- What do they think will help?
- What has held them back so far?

I've broken this down into five key areas for you to understand further what the process of 'sales' is:

1. ETHICS
The secret to great sales lies in identifying who you are best placed to support. Ethics serve as the guiding force, setting the tone for more authentic interactions and conversations. When you lead with ethics in sales, with the ultimate goal of reaching more people whose lives you can change, you attract more of the right people into your space.

2. SELLING THROUGH YOUR MESSAGE

The sales part becomes easier when you attract the right people and build a relationship with them before you consider the conversation part of the equation. Where a lot of entrepreneurs go wrong with their messaging is they make it about themselves and not their potential clients because they fear getting too specific and missing potential clients out. But speak to everyone, and you speak to no one.

Instead, focus on the messaging and language your dream clients will relate to. Get so specific with your messaging they are left nodding their heads. Your mission is to create posts that go from identifying a problem to offering a solution. The bit in between is where you show them why what they have done before didn't work.

People buy for different reasons, and we tap into that by having an equal split of content (blogs, social media, etc.) that educates your audience, connects with them through stories of your transformation and your clients and finally builds authority and trust by sharing proof of why you are credible and how you have helped others.

You are also not selling the vehicle through which they achieve their goal (e.g. a 6-week course or 90-minute 1:1); you are selling transformation. In each exchange, you're not just selling a product or service, but delivering something far more profound – clarity.

3. LISTENING

Sales conversations are not about giving them the answer, and this is where so many sales conversations go wrong. You should learn to listen in all touchpoints with potential clients such as the comments they leave on your social media posts, what they are posting themselves and responses you receive to offers. Focus on listening to what is shared. What are the gaps preventing them from getting to where they need to be? Think of your solutions as a tightrope between the two. You are the expert here, so it is for you to help them identify the real gap that is holding them back.

Sales should create an open and honest environment, which not only invites open dialogue so you can hear what future clients want and think they need but also lays the foundations for what it would be like to work together. If they tell you they are all in but don't share what might be holding them back, you may not have an environment of honesty and transparency, making it more difficult to support them.

If it's a given that you are leading with ethics, have taken time to understand what your dream clients want and are clear on the key transformation your service offers, then the first step of sales must come from listening. This ensures your solution is tailored to the individual.

4. URGENCY

The next part of effective sales is to identify how urgent the problem feels for them. If you are having conversations with people who have no more than an itch that they want to scratch, it is unlikely that working with you will get to the top of their list. We are living in a time of economic instability. This doesn't mean people aren't spending, but people need to be more certain about their decisions. Your content should do much of the sales objection handling for you and attract the right people to your calls.

If the number one objection you hear is price, clients are either not ready yet or do not see the value in what you can do. Your filtering process for who you have sales conversations with is as important as what happens on those calls. Limited time offers or limited spaces can also help create ethical tension which drives urgency.

5. YOUR SOLUTION

Once you have identified they are ready to make that change, with or without you (this is where the ethics part comes in), you are able to show what you feel is the best solution for them based on what they have shared. Be clear on what that will save them versus doing it themselves. It can be tempting to make assumptions based on budget, but you will speak to people who pay but didn't have the money to invest and people who had the money to invest but didn't buy.

You are the expert, so based on what you know and have heard, the next part of the sales conversation is the solution. Regardless of whether your dream client can afford it, you should offer the solution that is best for what they need. Not a menu of options that will overwhelm and lead to indecision.

Sound easy? Probably not, but eventually it does get easier, and in the meantime, it is more straightforward than you might think. If you understand your audience, what you write in your content and say when you speak to them will resonate. Do this with your unique personality and point of view (helping them differentiate and decide why you), and you make it easier for dream clients to recognise themselves in what you say.

In heart-led sales, the key isn't the 'gift of gab' but active listening, understanding gaps, and offering bespoke solutions. And those that step forward do so because now is the time. Urgency matters because it is about filtering in the right people for meaningful conversations. In a time when there is more demand for a more personalised approach, your unique approach and genuine listening will shape successful, heart-led sales.

In the next chapter, we will look at how to have more authentic sales conversations, more commonly known as sales calls.

CHAPTER 7

THE AUTHENTIC SALES CONVERSATION

If you are in any doubt about the need to evangelise about 'more heart, less hustle' when it comes to sales, think about the quick search of the term 'sales' I suggested earlier in the book. Type it in the search bar of any social media platform, and you'll likely see why I felt this book needed to be written. The loud sales coaches pacing on a stage with a headset on, sweat pouring down their brow as they shout instructions around lead chasing and closing a sale, will make you believe you need to adopt a loud, forceful demeanour. It is also why I still hear people tell me daily they 'aren't very salesy' or 'hate having to sell'.

Place yourself in a room full of successful entrepreneurs, and you will see that sales success doesn't have to be like that.

There is not one prototype for business success, and there is no one way to sell. I've built a career on heart-led sales, and at its core is the fundamental desire to help people and to choose people over numbers. Helping people is why I am still here, some three decades later, writing a book about sales.

Heart-led sales is at the crux of selling without the 'ick'. When you understand how to do it, you get to separate the price charged from your worth, because the two are not connected. You get to separate the outcome from the value of the conversation and attract people to your sales calls who have already decided.

Selling feels so much more aligned when you understand it is not about manipulating the outcome. Instead, it is a simple conversation. In this chapter, I will share with you the key things that stand in the way of generating more heart-led sales and what you can do to sidestep this to feel more aligned with conversations that lead to sales. Let's start with one of the most common things I see on sales calls – overtalking.

Who does most of the talking on your sales calls? Be honest, is it you? After all, why wouldn't you want to share the amazing ways you can transform someone's business? But if you are starting your calls talking about the history of your business, CV and credentials, you are most likely robbing yourself of vital information you need to know, which leads you to assumptions.

How many times have you been on a sales call, you get to the part of the call where you make an invitation, only for them to say no? They then share a vital piece of information which, if you had known, tells you they would not have been a match – all because you made an assumption.

Listening ensures you sidestep this and is one of the most accessible tools. People like to be heard as it leaves them feeling understood. Listening creates rapport, and from a psychological point of view activates the part of the brain connected with pleasure and reward. One of the ways to enable active listening on your sales calls is to ask specific questions that ensure you receive the information needed to help your dream client get closer to greater clarity.

Many sales coaches recommend scripts for sales calls, but that can cause anxiety as you navigate the script on a call. I suggest something I term the Authentic Sales Conversation. A short set of questions designed to get you from point A to B (the sales invitation) with what I call 'pit stops' along the way to ensure you can exit at any point if the call does not feel like a fit on either side. The questions are prompts to use during sales call with each taking you a step further. I've shared below the eight key questions I include in my Authentic Sales Conversation.

After a very brief introduction on the call about why they booked the call, which is a reminder of what was important to them in that moment, and what they do, this is the order of the key questions to ask. However, before you start the questions it's important to establish up front the objective of the call, which should be for them to make an empowered decision on the next steps and agree what that timeframe would look like. Once you have that clarity for you both, you can take them through the roadmap:

1. WHAT'S THE BIG VISION?
Here, you want to understand the big vision for the period shortly after you finish working together. Say, for example, you are working together for six months, what you want to understand is what they envisage for themselves a year from now. Ask them to expand on each point they share – what would that allow them to do? The idea is that they visualise what is possible for them.

2. WHERE ARE THEY NOW?
We don't start here because we don't want them to restrict their thinking by starting with where they currently are. Instead, you want them to start big with their future vision and then bring them to where they are now.

3. WHAT'S STANDING IN THE WAY OF REACHING THE FUTURE GOAL?
This question is designed to help highlight gaps between where they are now and where they want to be. This also gives you clarity on where they think the gaps are versus

what your experience and knowledge tell you. You are looking to identify how realistic their perception of the situation is. As the expert, one of your skills is being able to interpret what is being said by your dream client about what they are looking for. Sometimes what is being said is not a true reflection of what you might know they need. You can share observations on the real problem if you see it differently but be careful not to fall into the trap of advising on the call. The 'how' part is what your client pays you for, and it would be unfair to give advice without having all the information to make that assessment. Also, listen for what is shared here, as these are cues that will be key later. If, for example, they share that time is an issue, your most time intensive coaching programme may not be best suited to them.

4. WHY IS THIS (WHAT THEY HAVE SHARED AS THEIR BIGGEST OBSTACLE) A PROBLEM?

By understanding how significant the gap is between where they want to be and where they are now, you get to understand why change is important to them. This is helping you understand the cost of inaction, which you can reflect back to them when discussing how you can support them.

5. HOW DO YOU THINK I CAN HELP?

By reflecting their words and gaining micro-agreements throughout the conversations, you help them get clear on why and how you can help. Micro-agreements are a way of seeking their agreement throughout the conversation as you raise a point or bring clarity to something they have raised. This also creates greater certainty through the sales call that you have understood your potential client, there isn't a mismatch between their problem and your solution, and they agree with any reflections. This is something you can do throughout the call, but it is also worth a specific question to get them to reflect back to you their commitment to wanting to work with you and what they have understood.

6. HOW URGENT IS THE PROBLEM?

This is an important question because you want to understand how much of a priority this is for your client. This will indicate their willingness to commit and help you understand whether investing in support is a priority right now. If, for example, they are simply shopping around or gathering information, this would be a good point to use one of your pit stops. If they share that they are just shopping around for support later, you can signpost them to a lead magnet and suggest the conversation is continued when they are ready. An invitation to work with you may not be relevant for everyone, even if you have a call with them.

The idea of a sales call is not for your dream client to necessarily say yes but for them to have absolute clarity on the next steps they need to take in their business and whether they want to take this step with support. You want to help them to make an empowered decision. However, if the call is an information-gathering exercise, you won't need to get to the point of making an invitation. The clearer you and your dream client are throughout the call, the easier it is to understand the solution that will work best for them.

7. WHAT COULD STAND IN THE WAY OF DECIDING TO GET SUPPORT?

How willing is your dream client to be open to sharing information? This could be an indication of what it is like to work together. Therefore, you also want to understand what could stand in the way of making an empowered decision. What are the obstacles in their way? Are these real obstacles or simply masking fear?

8. SHALL I SHARE MORE ABOUT HOW I CAN SUPPORT YOU?

If your dream client has been open and shared information on the call that feels like a good match for your support, this is when you make an invitation to work together and look for an agreement in principle. I like to recommend you ascertain this before the price is shared, as you want to understand that if money was no object, does the solution you offer feel like a fit?

It is also about gaining an agreement that they can make that decision, either way, within an agreed time. Sitting in indecision is uncomfortable. That in combination with how likely they are to invest to buy are two key factors why decisions are best made close to the sales conversation, whilst still being respectful and mindful that people may have other factors to consider. The optimum time to decide to invest will be when they booked the call or on the call. The further away they get from the conversation, the more the propensity to invest will diminish. Acknowledge investing can feel scary and set the scene at the beginning of the call that this is about making an empowered decision, not just about saying yes.

What you want at the end of every sales call is to be clear about the three options available to everyone. The first option is to do nothing and for everything to stay the same, but with the added knowledge of how things could be different. This is why it is so important they can fully understand the cost of staying where they are. The second option is to make the changes but to do it themselves with the knowledge they now have. In this instance, what an expert provides is access, speed and expertise of the solutions they need. The third option is for them to work with you, with expertise, guidance, minimising risk and increasing the speed at which they reach their chosen result.

Sales calls can feel uncomfortable, so understanding the positioning of calls is key. Sales calls should not be offered to everyone, and not everyone on a sales call should get an offer. You want to make sure it is a fit for both them and you. Think about sales calls as an opportunity to connect with a dream client for your highest value offers, where you are offering the highest level of access to you. Greater clarity around the purpose of those sales calls helps your dream clients get clearer on the gap between where they want to be, where they are now and if you are the best person to help them get there.

When you start to reframe sales calls in this way, you'll shift any 'ick' you have associated with them. Now, let's look at what else might be getting in the way of greater, more effective conversions.

CHAPTER 8

CONFUSION KILLS CONVERSION

Confusion kills conversion. Read that again. Overwhelming people with too much information on sales calls is another one of the key reasons you aren't converting more of them.

There are two key instances where I see this happen. The first is if you start your sales call sharing all the incredible processes and techniques used to help your dream client get the results they desire. There is a danger this could subconsciously suggest you don't know what matters to who you are on the call with. It's also an overwhelming way to start a call at a point where you don't even know what they need. When you consider people will remember how you made them feel and not necessarily what you said (Brene Brown), you can see why starting your sales calls talking about logistics might miss the mark.

Be honest: how often do you spend a chunk of time at the beginning of your sales calls detailing how many sessions there are, what platform you use, where they can access the recording, what times of the day they can contact you between calls, etc.? It is overwhelming, and if, for example, they share later that time is an issue for them, you have just added to that feeling. Are you fearful of sounding 'too salesy' on your sales calls? Have you considered this could be because you are starting your calls talking about the exact steps your dream client will take when working with you – rather than focusing on what the steps lead to? If so, you're missing the mark.

Another sign you are spending too much time on the processes in your sales calls is your objections. I'll cover this fully later, but if you hear objections on sales calls, it can often be because your dream client didn't fully see the value in your offer. This is often triggered by too much focus on the process, and they can lose interest, leading them to disengaging. I always think of it as being like the first day of work in corporate and you're sitting in one of the many lengthy inductions where you take nothing in, and it's simply overwhelming. Sales calls can feel the same. Too much information leads to overwhelm or boredom, and that often leads to a no. No one wants to spend money on your offer if they have negative associations with your services.

CONFUSION KILLS CONVERSION

In the sales call roadmap we went through in the previous chapter, the questions included understanding how much of a priority this is for your dream client right now. That emotive reaction is when they consider if the transformation you offer is a match for the result they are looking for.

I am not saying don't talk about the features at all; just don't start with them on your sales calls. Instead, get clear on what your dream client wants at the end and remember the first question on the sales roadmap where you get them to envisage the big goal.

What your dream clients want to buy is clarity. To have that, they must understand what will be different at the end of their time working with you. This is why speaking to the right people is so important. It is not about having a huge number of followers or a massive launch – it's about the right people being crystal clear that your messaging is for them. The more you dilute the message, trying to be all things to all people, the more your messaging will land incorrectly.

Dream clients aren't buying the process. What they buy, based on emotional reasons, will be the transformation. Your dream clients want to picture what it will look like at the end for them. This is why your sales calls should help clients understand why they are more likely to get closer to their goal with you. They need assurance that working with an expert will be the most effective route to their end goal.

Logic is still important when making a buying decision,

especially a high-ticket one, as many will justify their buying decision with logic. What I am suggesting is starting your sales calls with transformation and not logic.

I know how important emotion is because I have seen it when working with clients who have sold out group programmes with no social media activity or email marketing. They achieved this result by simply having conversations with individuals with a problem that they knew they could help them with. Contrary to popular opinion, you don't always need fancy processes to make great sales. You just need to emotionally connect with your dream clients so they feel confident they will get closer to their end goal with you rather than without you.

The second way you are overwhelming clients on a sales call and killing conversion is by offering too many options of how to work with you. Too many choices are the equivalent of offering someone pages and pages of a Google search. If you don't know what they need after a 45-minute sales call, how can you expect them to?

Most people live in a world of choices, and we've become a society used to ease and speed, so overwhelming someone can happen fast when there are already more than 6000 pieces of information being taken in by them daily. Consider why, after a 45-minute sales call where your dream client has given you all the information you need to know, you are then giving them several choices. Is it because you fear rejection?

CONFUSION KILLS CONVERSION

Or are you making decisions about what to offer based on assumptions about their budget and your targets? Or to avoid an awkward conversation?

If so, you are setting yourself up to fail and not doing the best for your client. When you are on a sales call, you are the expert in what they need; therefore, you should be able to decide which option is best for them. Are you selling them what you think they can afford, what might be easiest to ask, or offering them what they need?

Always look at what your conversions data tells you. If you are getting 'noes' based, for example, on time commitment, consider what lies underneath this, which we will cover next.

CHAPTER 9

WHAT DOES THE DATA TELL YOU?

'Data is boring,' said many. But data is also the science behind sales. If stories are 'numbers with a heartbeat' then to have a great story, you must know your numbers. In the context of your sales calls, your numbers refer to how many calls convert to sales. Most often what stands in the way is objections. If you aren't having objections, you are most likely not having enough conversations.

Objections are rarely what you think they are and are not necessarily a no. What's shared as an objection often masks the real reason. More often than not, objections are used to avoid making a decision. Learning how to handle objections more effectively is not about forcing a sale, but considering what objections might be telling you.

Think about the most common objections on your sales calls. Are there patterns? If there are, this presents opportunities. By gathering this information, you can respond to the most common objections in your social media posts. Pre-empting common objections through your content also means that they are handled ahead of calls, leading to better conversions. As I have previously shared, not everyone gets a call or invitation to work with you. It has to be a fit before you get to this point.

I also want you to think about your role on a sales call and that includes your mindset – you are on the call as an expert in the area they need help with. Regardless of whether they are the CEO of a huge corporation or the founder of a small business, they are having a conversation with you because you have the expertise they are looking for. If objections leave you feeling deflated on calls, it's often a sign you are misdirected in how you see them.

Objections aren't necessarily roadblocks. As well as being a method of avoiding a decision, they can also be a sign your potential client hasn't fully grasped the offer or that you are speaking to someone who isn't a match. This misunderstanding can stem from various factors, such as a lack of clarity on the call, engaging with the wrong audience or insufficiently explaining the benefits of your solution. Objections can also signal a lack of trust or confidence that what you have shared will get your dream client closer to their goal. Sometimes an objection is simply fear.

Acknowledge during the conversation that it is scary to make a big commitment to yourself (let alone the money they will spend), and it's normal to feel fear. There can also be the fear it won't work or that they will be the ones who can't make it work. That's why establishing trust not only on the call but before it is important – and through your content, which we will cover.

An objection means you are still in communication with your potential client. It's an opportunity to help them understand their objection, and what it might indicate.

On a call, ensure you are using the prompts from Chapter 7 to help you understand how best to help them. Listen for the main objections that might come up on a sales call. Below are some of the most common ones and what you should consider when handling these objections:

1. 'I NEED TO THINK ABOUT IT'

With high-ticket coaching this is a valid consideration, but consider the peak points at which there is a desire to achieve the result you offer. This is why I recommend seeking agreement during the call that they will decide on how they will achieve their next steps, on which you have given clarity, within an agreed time. If at the end of the call they share they need more time to consider, acknowledge it is a big decision, but ask what the main thing is they need to consider. This allows you to understand if this is something you can help with.

Consider ethical tension here with your offers as that also helps people make calls based on availability, times or limited bonus offers. If, for example, they share a fear of it not working, a money-back guarantee may help. You need to know their objection before you offer what may help them decide.

2. 'I DON'T HAVE THE MONEY / I CAN'T AFFORD IT'

If this keeps coming up, you may need to consider who you are attracting, the format of your sales calls, when you make offers, what evidence it is based on, or using pre-qualifying questions. When this comes up on a call, I like to ask if money was put aside, how clear are they that the promise shared is where they want to be?

The response helps you identify if the real issue is money or if this is a mask for something else. Sometimes it's easier for potential clients to hide behind 'money' but more often it's masking something else, which could include a lack of clarity in the result or even trust in themselves that it will work. I'm not saying money is never the reason, but most often it is not.

This objection is also an opportunity to explore the cost of inaction. My recommendation is to discuss this in your content and on the call, as one of the questions is about their future vision. If that is where they want to be, what is the cost of not getting there to them? Because you want to identify here whether the issue is budget. More often, it is perceived value or their belief it will not work.

If the objection is budget, consider whether a payment plan would be beneficial and what might the cost be further down the line if they wait? Doing nothing will not mean the problem remains the same, as in a few months they will be even further behind. Sometimes it is about the price, but what price would they invest at? In many instances if you ask this, you won't hear a figure, but the real reason behind their objection.

3. 'I NEED TO CHECK WITH MY PARTNER'

What's important to acknowledge here is that sometimes there is a genuine need to discuss with a business partner or life partner, as they are either involved in the decision-making process or finances. Identify this earlier in the sales call when you understand what has held them back so far from moving forward, or what else they need to consider to step forward. A question you can ask if this objection comes up is, 'What do you think your partner will need to know to help you make that decision?'

You also want to keep in mind that ultimately the best conversations will happen when you have all the decision-makers in a room, so make an offer to jump on another call at a time that works for both of them. This allows you to convey the important information to everyone rather than rely on them passing the information on. If they are not in agreement to do that, ask what their decision would be if their partner said no.

These questions may feel uncomfortable at first but remember you want to work with someone you can have an open and honest conversation with so they can make the decision that's best for them. This is always about the best decision, not making a sale. That said, if this objection keeps coming up for you, consider who you are attracting, where they are in their journey and how empowered they are to make the decision on investing.

4. 'I AM SPEAKING TO SOME OTHERS AS WELL'

As I shared previously, not everyone gets a sales call or an offer. The offer should be made where there is a fit. There are points throughout the sales call that, if it doesn't feel like a fit, you can exit the call and perhaps direct them to a free resource or your content. However, if you have made an offer and they have shared this is a priority for them right now, but they need to speak to other coaches, consider if this is a delaying tactic. Also, consider if they are 'shopping around', because then this isn't a sales call, it is an information-gathering exercise.

You will have gained agreement at the beginning of the sales roadmap if they are looking to make an empowered decision within an agreed time. You do that not just because indecision is uncomfortable but because the conversation you are having is based on what is available now, including your capacity and the current investment. If they say they are also speaking to others, ask them what has resonated the most from what you have shared and what else they are still hoping to find. This creates an open dialogue on the call. If this objection comes up, acknowledge that you understand and explain how what you do is not comparable, including your unique blueprint that distinguishes you from others in the market. The 'offer' is the last part of the call. So, if they have shared they are shopping around, it would not be relevant to make an offer. Instead, be clear why you are not comparable and invite them to speak to others and come back to you if they do not find what they are looking for.

5. 'NOW IS NOT THE TIME'

Often, when this comes up, they are saying that this doesn't feel like a priority for them right now. It's one of the reasons I do not recommend you start your sales calls with the intricacies of the process, as it can be overwhelming and so much more than they may have been looking for. If they share that now does not feel like the time, empathise with them and acknowledge what they have said. Clarify what made them get in touch and ask what has led them to believe that now is not the time.

This is a reminder of the gap between where they are and where they wanted to be. Also, acknowledge that it is a commitment but that is why you have designed your service in this way – so it doesn't feel overwhelming, and they are supported. Consider your audience here too. Are they information seekers happy to take the information and do it themselves, or are they knowledge seekers looking to be shown how it will be done?

6. 'I WILL GET BACK TO YOU IN A FEW DAYS'

You want to be clear about what the biggest consideration is, and this might be something you can help them with there and then.

Remember, the start of any sales conversation is an agreement that the purpose of the sales call is for them to get clarity on their next steps and make an empowered decision, ideally within twenty-four or forty-eight hours of the call. Remind your client it will be uncomfortable for them to be stuck in indecision and share that the propensity for them to buy will diminish the further they are from the call.

This isn't about making a sale, but supporting your potential clients to make the decision that is best for them whilst they have all the information fresh in their minds, and for you as the expert to support them with this. Availability, pricing and what they need will also change in the future. Therefore, the call is based on the current needs and status of both sides. Your role is to be clear on how you will support them best to make that decision in an agreed amount of time.

Armed with this information, I invite you to get curious next time you are on a sales call, understand the reason behind the objections, and consider it an opportunity to support your clients in finding the best decision for them. Objections are the evidence you need to understand what support a potential client requires to decide.

Whilst sales calls are a fundamental part of making more sales, content also plays a big part. In the final part of the book, we will consider how to create messaging that attracts more of your dream clients to your social media, blogs or websites, connecting with these potential clients and finally converting them, doing much of the heavy lifting of sales for you.

TASK 3: OBJECTION HANDLING

How often do you look at the data behind your sales calls and conversations? How aware are you of what is standing in the way of your potential dream client working with you? These core objections are key to understanding your audience, whether you are speaking to the right people, and the perfect foundation for your messaging.

Gather data based on your last ten sales conversations and the next five you have. This may take time if you haven't recorded past calls, so go through emails and notes that may have been written after the calls. Use the information from these interactions to uncover the potential client's primary objections. This exercise will help you understand their concerns, sharpen your skills in empathetic listening and objection handling, help you get comfortable in the DMs, have sales conversations, and even hear 'no'. A pro tip: going forward, record all your sales calls. You can start by letting them know you record calls so that you don't miss anything. It's always useful to watch calls back to pick up nuances and review how the call went.

Once you have this list, plan five pieces of content that speak to your dream client's main objections and address common concerns. Use the content to do the heavy lifting and get you more confident handling those objections on your next sales call. The steps are outlined below:

1. Collect Data

Objective: Gather detailed information from your sales conversations.

Action: Review your last ten sales conversations and the next five you have. Check emails, notes, and any post-call reflections to extract key points about your client's pain points, desires, objections, and recurring concerns.

2. Analyse Insights

Objective: Identify common themes.

Action: Now group the most common points shared on calls and messages. Look for patterns in the challenges clients face, their desires and note recurring themes. This helps pinpoint the most pressing concerns and future focus of your dream clients.

3. Plan Content

Objective: Create targeted content that addresses objections.

Action: Using insights from your analysis, plan five pieces of content. Each piece should directly address a key objection or concern (or desire) that came up in conversations. Aim to provide solutions, offer reassurance, and show empathy. Get specific in your examples of how these show up in your dream clients' daily lives.

4. Test Your Messaging

Objective: Refine your approach based on real interactions and use it to extend conversations from comments under the post into the DMs.

Action: As you create and share your content, pay attention to how your audience responds. Use feedback and engagement to adjust your messaging, ensuring it resonates with your dream clients and effectively addresses their concerns. If your dream clients send you screenshots of your posts and stories on social media asking to find out more, you're on the right path. If they aren't, how can you make your messaging resonate more?

5. Refine Sales Conversations

Objective: Improve your objection-handling skills.

Action: Use what you've learned to refine your approach in future sales conversations. With time you'll have gained greater experience, for example, of the most common objections and begun to address these in your content regularly.

WHAT DOES THE DATA TELL YOU?

6. Review and Reflect

Objective: Deepen your understanding and improve your strategy.

Action: At the end of this process, review your data and insights. Reflect on how these conversations and content pieces have enhanced your understanding of your dream clients. Use this knowledge to continually refine your sales approach, content strategy, and client interactions.

PART 3

SALES ATTRACTION

CHAPTER 10

STORYSELLING THROUGH CONTENT

Social media isn't always a good thing. Yet it gives you access to billions of people globally and if used well, for example through curating your feed, you have access at your fingertips to a significant number of potential dream clients. In this part of the book, I'll share the role your social media content has in attracting, connecting and converting more dream clients online and how to craft content that does most of the heavy lifting of sales for you. Your audience is watching you through your social media content, even if you don't always know it, which makes it a powerful platform for sales attraction.

If someone were to scroll through your search history on social media and ask you to recall details about what you have seen, most likely, you would not remember them. What you might remember, though, are the stories shared. Storytelling is about taking facts and transforming how they are conveyed through your words. This is why digital content that leaves a positive impression on the reader and emotionally connects has the biggest impact on dream clients.

Let's put this into practice. How often do you meet online contacts offline and not remember their company name or even their surname but recall a detail they share about themselves or their mission through their content? For most of us, this is highly likely to be the case. This is why when it comes to your content and messaging (on social media, websites, blogs, etc.), what you want it to be is:

- **Memorable**
- **Consistent**
- **Clear**
- **Interesting**
- **Useful**

I'll go into detail on these later in the chapter.

Content that helps with sales attraction is not limited to written content; your messaging is also about what your brand says through video, positioning, collaboration, etc. Digital platforms offer several ways to share your brand story and engage with your audience, and short-form video is one of the most effective ways of connecting with them.

With online digital content, how social media is formatted, the number of characters you are given and the length of the videos all show you need to present your content in a particular way for it to be simple, digestible and memorable. Most of the digital marketing gurus recommend you write for a 6th grader (10 to 11-year-old), and that's not easy, especially with backgrounds in corporate!

But great content has to capture attention. Social media platforms, such as LinkedIn, algorithmically reward content where the audience clicks to see more after the first two lines of a post by then showing your content to more people. To do this, make it interesting while not giving it all away in the first few lines. And so begins the power of learning how to effectively tell a story through messaging.

It is the same for video content; an audience usually decides if they want to watch more within seconds. Therefore, your opening line must be compelling, which usually works best when you speak to a pain point, a key consideration when you are looking to attract dream clients. In sales, pain points refer to a specific problem or challenge that your potential customers face. Identifying these pain points is crucial because it allows you to tailor your products or services to address and alleviate these issues. But key here is the importance your potential client places on their pain point.

It is usually more than a minor inconvenience, or at least something they are prioritising. Once you've pinpointed pain points, tailor your messaging to show how your solutions directly address and solve these problems. Remember, it's about empathy and providing genuine solutions rather than simply pushing a product or service. By acknowledging and addressing the pain points your audience experiences, you're better positioned to share specific examples they can relate to on how this shows up. With more experienced clients these problems or pain points can be replaced by desires.

The foundation of great storytelling through your content, like all great stories, is that it has a beginning, middle and end, with each section giving the audience a reason to continue. But unlike a book or essay, you have to get to the point in far fewer characters in digital content.

Great stories can also be told in different ways, which is where content length and formats come into play to appeal to the various ways your audience likes to absorb information and the different types of buyers. Content also takes your audience on a journey, which is why you will hear about creating content that builds 'know, like and trust' with them.

For the vast majority of you (including me), the work you do is not unique – you are one of many. This is not necessarily a negative, as it means there is a proven market. And as many business gurus say there is more than enough business and people to go around. When you are one of one, this can mean it's either a service that has not been proven to have demand yet or it is not a viable offer as it was tried and failed by others before you. If you are one of many though, you want to identify what makes you different. Therefore, what you are doing through your messaging is creating distinction, and the most distinct thing about you is you. This is why creating stories around your experience is the most compelling way to create content that connects with more of your dream clients.

Here is the other thing about great stories – they get shared. How many times has a friend or peer mentioned, 'Did you see the story about ...'? Through your content, great stories will be useful not only to the reader but also possibly to the reader's network, which is why you need to be clear about your objectives with your audience. If your goal is to reach more people by having content shared, ask them to reshare it if they find it interesting. You want to make it as simple as possible for people to take action.

Simplifying social media content is important because of the limited attention span of online users. Dwell time is also shorter as people are scrolling, so key messages appeal to this simplicity as they make it easier to make a decision. And that saves busy people time!

Taking this one step further, with the goal of building content that attracts more dream clients, an adaptation of the term storytelling is to consider how your content is

StorySelling. A phrase I coined is The Art of StorySelling®.

Writing compelling content as a business owner might not be everyone's forte, and that's okay. But understanding the purpose, potential and power of social media reach might help you decide whether this is something you want to improve considering how beneficial it can be to growing the sales in your business. While having an online business that resonates with dream clients and drives sales doesn't solely rely on social media, it's hard to ignore that the online world boasts a global audience of billions. For most entrepreneurs, dismissing the sales opportunity of content and messaging through social media might be a missed trick.

StorySelling helps as a strategic approach that intertwines storytelling with a clear end goal: making sales. It's about consciously shaping what you want to be known for, resonating with how your audience feels, and driving specific actions. In essence, it's storytelling with a sales purpose.

To break it down further, the objective of your content is to connect with your dream client. You want your content to feel relatable and become a catalyst for action – whether stepping into your DMs, engaging with content, sparking curiosity, or even making a transaction.

Effective StorySelling creates a more seamless shift, making your dream client feel that the story could be about them. This connection happens when you understand and speak to your audience. Relatable stories, transformations, and experiences shared from your position of expertise and experience allow your dream client to see how you can help and why you're the best person for this. This, in turn, supports a more heart-led approach to sales, which is at the crux of what I have taught for over three decades, and the heart of this book.

StorySelling creates content that acts as a bridge between you and your dream client. It's not just about sharing information, but creating an emotional connection with real impact. Even something simple, such as a like, comment, or share, signifies a step closer to building a community around your brand.

Great StorySelling also provides solutions. Your content positions you as the expert who not only understands your dream client's challenges but gives them insight into how this can change for them. This creates a narrative where your dream client not only sees themselves in the story but considers how you can help them.

Writing good content isn't about being a copywriter – it is about understanding how the platform you are on presents your information and how the reader is digesting it. Creating clarity around who you are, who you are for and how you help will support you in producing content that ultimately supports and builds your business so you value the time you spend online. Whilst AI is valuably integrated on most platforms now, what is crucial here is not to lose sight of what is uniquely you and how to use it to enhance what you pour into any AI that you might use to support content creation. Trust is built through authenticity, which includes your content.

As you see, great sales begin long before the final transaction. And how you connect with your audience is key.

Let's dive further into the key points shared at the beginning of this chapter about what makes great content – StorySelling that connects with your audience at a deeper level – before we move on to your sale's 'voice' in the next chapter.

MEMORABLE:

Craft content that leaves a lasting impression by becoming the storyteller who stops the scroll.

This can be done effectively through compelling stories that resonate emotionally with your audience. By sharing relatable experiences and weaving a narrative into your content, you become the storyteller who stops the scroll. Engage your audience's emotions, making your brand and messages more memorable.

CONSISTENT:

Consistency is paramount. Reinforce key messages consistently, allowing your brand's essence to be obvious while remembering only a small percentage of people will see a specific piece of content and an even smaller percentage will remember it. StorySelling allows you to reinforce key messages consistently through storytelling. This lets you repeat a message in many ways, without it feeling repetitive. By incorporating your brand's essence into narratives, you create a consistent thread through your content. While understanding that not everyone sees every piece of content, StorySelling ensures that the core messages are reiterated, increasing the chances of them being remembered and relevant. The more often your content feels relevant, the more your audience will return to it, and the clearer the algorithm will be about who your content serves.

CLEAR:
Cut through the noise with crystal-clear messaging. Aim not just to convey but connect. In an era inundated with information, keep it simple. Use StorySelling to cut through the noise and deliver crystal-clear messages.

INTERESTING:
Visibility is not enough; strive to be interesting. Your content should start with a hook, leaving your audience curious enough to 'see more'. StorySelling empowers you to begin your content with a narrative that intrigues and increases the likelihood of holding your audience's attention in a sea of competing information.

USEFUL:

Beyond being a digital library, use StorySelling to offer value. Share insights, provide valuable information, and position yourself as the go-to expert in your subject area. StorySelling enables you to seamlessly integrate useful content into your narratives, making your stories not only engaging but also beneficial to your audience. To write great content, which attracts more dream clients, understand how to connect with them so that they grow to know, like and trust you.

As well as knowing what to write, it's also important to develop your distinctive voice through your content, which we will cover next.

CHAPTER 11

CREATING TONE THROUGH MESSAGING

WHY ARE YOU SHOUTING? I'm not; I just forgot to turn the caps lock off. Yet, it's a common thought when people see text written in capital letters. Writing in capitals isn't the only way to convey tone, and written words are not the only way to create tone in your messaging. Tone becomes your sales voice, distinguishing you from others.

Understanding the role of social media content is crucial to knowing how to give it a starring role in your sales process. Sales is easier when you have attracted more of the right clients to you; building connections will feel more authentic, and conversion will follow more naturally. This is why getting the tone right is an important factor in who you want to attract.

I often remind my clients and audience on social media that there is a reason the digital landscape is seeing such growth in the popularity of short-form video content. They dominate social media because of how they can be easily absorbed, which taps into shorter attention spans and mobile usage. Most people access social media apps through their mobile, often whilst on the move and multi-tasking, all of which impacts how they like to absorb content. Moreover, you get to hear how someone sounds, their intonation, and watch their movements, which adds to the tone of the content. The combination of seeing and hearing a person can create a deeper connection.

Tone helps create an environment that attracts more of your dream clients, and it is an important part of the know, like and trust factor, which in turn will increase the likelihood of making sales with the right people for your business.

With sales, social media and the digital landscape play a crucial role in building genuine connections between your business and audience. Connection is more than just the part where you sell your service; it creates a space where your audience feels a personal connection with you and your brand. This is especially important where you are one of many doing what you do. Here are just some of the ways you can master tone through your content.

CREATING TONE THROUGH MESSAGING

1. UNDERSTANDING YOUR AUDIENCE

Since hearing the quote 'Masters never don't do the basics', by marketing guru Alex Hormozi, I've not stopped using it. No matter where you are in business, whether looking to reach the next level or simply trying to get started, you must get clear on and often revisit the foundations, in this case, understanding your audience.

If you can understand what your audience feels, needs and says, what you create will speak to their problem, desire or pain point. These have to be more than a minor inconvenience as it has to be something they are willing to invest in. This also goes beyond the demographics into the psychographics, which delves into the psychological and lifestyle traits of a target audience. They include factors such as values, interests, attitudes, behaviours, hobbies, and beliefs, which all help you speak directly to your dream client.

Once you understand your audience, even down to their language, you can consider the tone that resonates with them best. Not every sales mentor will promote niching your target audience, and it is not relevant for every business. But for most of you, having some commonality in the people you are speaking to will be incredibly useful as this allows you to tailor your messaging and attract people who resonate with your content. Niching has long since moved along from the more traditional segmentation of audience by age, location and/or gender.

2. REFLECTING ON YOUR BRAND PERSONALITY

Your brand has its distinctive personality – traits that should set it apart from the rest. Whether it's friendly, professional, direct, or humorous, let these traits radiate through your social media content. Allow the unique characteristics of your brand to shine in your tone, creating a voice that resonates with your dream clients. One of the ways you can do this is to have three or four personal pillars running alongside your business brand pillars. Think of this as personalisation as they are the themes of your personal story that are relevant not only to your business but also to your audience. People buy people, so consider how your brand represents you.

How you write, speak and even visually portray your brand will also support reflecting your brand personality. For example, if your brand exudes a friendly and approachable style, infusing this tone into your social media content can make it feel more relatable. In turn, this creates a deeper connection with those who relate to it, and they will feel like they know you.

3. CONSISTENCY

If someone scrolls through your social media, visits your website, reads your blogs and looks at your digital footprint via a search engine, how consistent would your tone be? While each platform has its distinctive personality and, dare

I say, 'vibe', your messaging should still deliver a recognisable brand experience.

This approach reinforces brand recognition and cultivates trust and familiarity among your audience. Ways that you can do this can include the terms that you use, brand colours and anchoring your messaging in three or four core pillars so the messaging and what you are 'famous for' becomes super clear.

4. CREATE CONTENT THAT SHOWS THEM WHY

Consider the point behind your content, your 'why'. Why are you wanting your message to reach more people? One of the ways you can do this, like a litmus test, is to ask yourself 'So what?' when reviewing content, as this is what creates greater depth and relevancy. Relevancy makes what you have shared feel more memorable and creates a deeper bond with your audience.

When you consider tone, speak to your audience not just as numbers but heartbeats. This lends itself to building a community as you develop a deeper connection. This intentional and personable tone transforms the information you are sharing into a genuine connection, inviting your audience to not only understand the 'why' but emotionally align with it.

5. ADAPTING TO THE PLATFORM

Different platforms have different rules of engagement. Tailor your tone to fit each platform while maintaining your brand voice. For instance, the professional tone suitable for LinkedIn might not resonate as well with the more casual and creative space of TikTok.

One way to do this is to consider the mindset of the audience when they arrive on that platform. Yes, the audiences can differ across the platforms, but there is also the case of the same person being on different platforms. How might they be showing up on those platforms differently? For example, are they in a more fun, frivolous mood on TikTok? Are they looking for inspiration on Instagram and Pinterest? Or for education on YouTube and insights and business conversations on LinkedIn? Your content's tone should be distinctly you, drawing on different aspects of your personality, but should also meet your audience where they are at, showing them how you can help them get to the level they aspire to.

6. SHOWCASING AUTHENTICITY

Authenticity is the anchor of trust-building in the digital landscape. It's not about just sharing the highs and lows, but sharing how that helps your audience and how that shaped what you know now. Openness and truth can cultivate a connection with your audience beyond just being visible so that you can make money. It has the power to humanise your brand and create a deeper bond with your audience.

Authenticity is about being real and relatable, letting your audience see the people and stories behind your brand. This transparency fosters trust as audiences appreciate businesses that are open and honest about their experiences.

Consider your core personal pillars and how this feeds into your content, such as integrating personal stories and experiences into your content. This includes behind-the-scenes glimpses or anecdotes reflecting the values and ethos of your brand. Authenticity is not about showcasing perfection, but embracing imperfections and the human side of your business. Authenticity creates a tone of openness and relatability, while showing the human side of the business.

However, approach your openness with a filter and a degree of caution. Ask yourself how this is relevant to your brand and business and what it will tell your audience about you. For example, sharing that you are having a difficult time might create concern with potential clients if you are a coach. But showing in retrospect how you overcame a challenge and what this taught you might feel more valuable.

And finally, be mindful of inauthentic authenticity, crying on camera is very different to crying for the camera, and there have been well-known influencers and businesses who have attempted to manufacture genuineness for marketing purposes. Audiences are adept at discerning sincerity, and inauthentic authenticity can lead to a loss of trust.

7. USING VISUALS STRATEGICALLY

A bad visual can be as harmful to your brand as bad copy. I like to ask my clients to consider how believable they think their business is. If you were to arrive on your page and see the quality of your visuals, what would you think? Would you invest in you?

Tone can be created through lighting, high-quality images, engaging videos, or eye-catching graphics. However, avoid stock library images as they take away personalisation, which will impact your connection with your audience. Strategically using visuals enhances the overall impact of your content. And yes, as a business owner, unless you outsource, you do have to master many skills, but tools such as Canva make creating visuals a whole lot easier.

Crafting the perfect tone in your content is an ongoing journey. It involves understanding your audience, maintaining consistency, and infusing authenticity into your brand's personality. By utilising engaging strategies like storytelling, humour, and visuals, you can create a deeper connection with your audience. Once you've attracted the right people to your content, you can connect (nurture and build a community) and finally convert. And this is where we will go next.

CHAPTER 12

CONNECTION TO CONVERSION

Since the pandemic, online businesses have seen huge growth. The shift to remote working and changes in consumer behaviour have driven business owners to explore digital avenues, leading to a boom in e-commerce, online coaching and digital services. This shift has accelerated the importance of establishing an online presence, not just having a social media account but using it to support building your profile and attracting more dream clients. However, with increased opportunities come new challenges, including competition for you.

As coaches in the online space, it's about finding a balance between being more visible whilst still creating a business that leads with authentic, heart-led sales. Creating a genuine connection with your audience is not only strategically beneficial, but makes the sales process so much more principled.

In the previous chapters, I shared the role content plays in helping you attract more of your dream clients. In this chapter, I'll be taking you deeper into the intricacies of leveraging content and social media to not only connect with but ultimately convert more of your dream clients.

First consider how to make your dream audience stay once you have attracted more of them to your content. One of the best ways is to make your content more relevant to them more of the time. What do they have in common? And this isn't just about gender and age. What are their beliefs? And once you know this, how does this allow you to target your message more precisely? These insights become the foundation to build a meaningful connection through your content so your dream client hears and sees themselves in what you say repeatedly.

Authenticity is a key pillar for any successful coach or creative online, particularly where you are not meeting your audience in real life. Your content should not merely represent your business values but echo your ethos. The core business and personal pillars we have already touched upon will become the cornerstones around which your content is created and humanise your brand.

Transparency through your digital content can also support connection and your audience getting to know, like and trust you and your brand. Speak directly to the experiences of your audience, letting them know they are not alone in their challenges and successes. What will make your audience stay is the consistency of your message, its relevance to them and content that not only educates but also builds your authority as the go-to expert in that area. This is what takes your audience on a journey to getting closer to being your client.

There is a reason why there is more than one social media platform and these platforms offer content in more than one format. People do not absorb information in the same way. Diversification is key in capturing different preferences of the people you want to be seen by. Incorporate a mix of blogs, text-only posts, longer articles, visually engaging infographics, captivating videos, and thought-provoking podcasts to attract your potential audience because not everyone has the same preferences or attention spans.

But you also don't have to do it all. Consider what suits you best and what the data and insights (yes, that again) tell you about what your audience likes best. The most important numbers you should focus on is which type of content leads to deeper conversations off the page in the DMs and on clarity calls.

Whilst different platforms lend themselves better to different formats, you should still deliver a consistent brand voice (tone) across platforms. This establishes trust in the online space. From colour schemes to tone of voice, a unified appearance builds recognition and identity for your brand.

Consistency also helps create trust, which is key in turning browsers into buyers. And how your brand looks will leave an impression.

Does your visual content look streamlined? Is your video clear, and fonts aligned? Or does it look like a DIY school project? What impression will that leave when conversations turn to the cost of working with you? Investing in your content visuals doesn't have to start as a large sum and many free tools are available. But you do need to be clear about who your brand is for, what your brand says and how you want your brand to be received. If it looks like a business owner isn't consistent in showing up online and doesn't have synergy in how their brand appears online, what impression might this give to someone looking to invest?

The next dynamic in taking dream clients from arriving on your page to connecting with you on a more personal level is the 'social' part of social media! Don't post and ghost. You may have heard that term before, and it is about social media being exactly that – social. The platforms have been designed to encourage usage, add value through their users and build communities. Social media platforms give you direct access to your audience, and authenticity in engagement involves responding to comments, posing questions, and actively participating in discussions. To make it meaningful, ask yourself where you add value and position yourself as the expert in your field whilst still respecting others who are the experts in theirs.

This isn't about mindlessly scrolling. It's about being intentional with your time and where you are hanging out. Setting aside time to coincide with when your post goes live can be an effective way of alerting your followers (and, dare I say it again, the algorithm) that you are active. Understandably, many of you have a love-hate relationship with social media. It can seem time-consuming and no doubt frustrating if you don't see the results, but this is almost always not about doing more on social media but getting the foundations in place and being consistent and intentional with your time.

One way of making what you share more memorable and create a stronger bond with your audience is through personal stories and your clients' stories. Examples of your clients' successes, emphasising the transformative impact your products or services have had on their lives, can be interwoven into stories. Weaving narratives that align with the aspirations and challenges of your dream clients enables them to see themselves in the stories you tell. This takes your audience on more of a journey than sharing a testimonial or review, although they also have a place in connecting with your dream clients and cutting though social media noise.

In the digital age, social proof can be powerful in influencing your dream client's decisions. Similar to storytelling, this allows your potential audience to see people 'like them'. Feature testimonials and reviews on your website and social media channels. Nothing says it better than word of mouth or hearing it directly from someone. Social proof allows you to create that same sentiment.

Encourage satisfied clients to share their experiences, showcasing the tangible impact your offerings have on their lives. Social proof can be a potent endorsement that can also influence a potential client towards conversion. However, don't just share or post a screenshot of the results your client received – accompany this with a story of what can be achieved when your dream client gets support around a specific area.

Your content should be informative so your audience returns to it, known as 'sticky' content, and include educational content, which is often your 'how to' content. However, this is not about positioning your content just as a library, but you as an authority and expert. You can do this by consistently delivering valuable and educational content.

Address common pain points, share industry insights, and offer practical tips that resonate with your dream client. This shows them what you know, how you know it, and how it will help. It also serves your community with free content while providing a taste of what they would get if they worked with you. The more you position yourself as a source of knowledge and support, the more your audience views the transformation from your service as an essential solution to their needs.

To rely on social media content alone to build your business and convert your audience would be dangerous. Do you remember the last time Facebook went down? Or LinkedIn stopped working? Both are examples from not so long ago, and a reminder to many in the online world about the importance of building a community in more than one place. In other words, don't put all your eggs in one basket.

You want an army of loyal supporters, and email marketing remains a powerful tool for cultivating relationships with potential clients. Craft newsletters that add value and offer exclusive content that caters to the specific needs and interests of subscribers. How many are being opened, and how many links are being clicked on? This will give you a guide of what to do more or less to connect and convert dream clients.

Another way to build a deeper connection with your online audience outside of your social media content might include communication with your most loyal 'fans' through messaging apps including WhatsApp updates, as an addition or even alternative to an email subscriber list. This is an additional way to reach and engage with your community, who may not all necessarily be paying clients.

In recent times, there has been an increase in the use of SMS for nurturing customer relationships. As there is an increase in business chat over SMS and big businesses are building it into their ways of communicating with their customer bases, it has become more of a familiar way of communicating. One key advantage of including SMS in communicating with your audience is the ability to create instant connection. Text messages are more likely to be read and responded to promptly, providing a swift and direct line of communication.

Research has shown a greater attendance rate for masterclasses when SMS reminders are used. I would, however, approach with caution as not every demographic has reacted as favourably to SMS by businesses, so it is important to understand who your audience is and how they will react. It's also crucial to use SMS with integrity. I accept it for my consumer purchases and services, but I don't like its use in the coaching space. What do your dream clients think about it? Overuse or irrelevant messages may lead to turning off your audience and impact trust.

Content and social media can be powerful in building a deeper connection with your dream clients. Through genuine connections, you can navigate the digital landscape with greater ease and purpose and empower your audience to make informed and confident decisions.

TASK 4: CONDUCT A MINI AUDIT

Now you have a greater understanding of the role of content in driving sales, I invite you to look at your last 30 pieces of sales content and do a mini audit. This could be social media content and include blogs from your website. This audit will allow you to see the role your content has played to date – have you been turning up as an online library, bearing your soul, showing up as a blogger or have you got the temperature right.

For this task, I would like you to categorise your content into four key areas: Authority and Trust, Inspire and Connect, Educate and Inform and Pure Sales Post. Doing this will allow you to consider at a glance where your content might be skewed.

Categorise your last 30 pieces of content and assess if the purpose of the content is to:

Educate and Inform: 'How to' content _____ %

Inspire and Connect: Stories of
transformation, including your own
and clients _____ %

Build Authority and Trust: Proof of
your creditability and knowledge of the
area, which could include testimonials
and collaborations with other partners   _____ %

Pure Sales Post: Where you are selling
a specific service   _____ %

Next to each one, write the percentage that sits against each category. You will notice some posts cross over more than one category. If so, choose the more dominant category.

You want to create content that takes your audience on a journey to understand how you can help, why they should work with you and how they can make that happen. By having content that taps into the reasons someone might buy, you also build a deeper connection with your audience and foster community, which will support you in building the trust that leads to more authentic conversations in your comments and DMs. The more relevant what you share is, the more likely your conversation will lead to conversion on sales calls.

CHAPTER 13

THE GOLD IS IN THE REPETITION

How can you bring more heart and less hustle into your sales approach? Hopefully, by now, you have understood that this starts with reframing how you see sales. Traditionally, sales has been associated with relentless hustle, but where we are now is that heart-led sales are transforming the way people do business, which resonates at a deeper level with a society that is increasingly focused on human connection and consciousness.

I've seen first-hand how reframing sales can be powerful. I recently worked with a client who is a business coach. Her signature offer was a high ticket, high touch group programme. She was attracting lots of people into her funnel, which was a masterclass, but her conversion rates were low.

When we spoke about this, it was evident not everyone who came through on a call was at the right level for the programme and that she didn't enjoy sales calls. We looked at her content messaging to identify what level of client she attracted, and then at the qualifying process to ensure her sales calls were with the right people.

Alongside this was understanding the purpose of a sales call, as we touched on earlier in the book. It is not to get a sale, but identify a fit. Offers only get made when you get to the part of the call when both sides can see the fit. When we last spoke, she told me the work we have done means she is now converting four out of every five sales calls. She now loves the process, and if they aren't a fit, the call does not extend to an offer. That's how powerful a more heart-led approach to sales can be in your business.

Sales isn't just a tool. As we have seen, it is about understanding how crucial a role sales plays in helping people have access to a service that solves a problem, but also helps the business offering that solution grow and be able to reinvest back into their business. Your view of the function of sales may have been formed early in life, and how you find sales will almost certainly be impacted by your thoughts around it. You can impact your business's sales by changing how you approach it and understanding what your dream client needs. This reflects in your messaging and who that attracts. Sales are about building that community of people who know, like, and trust you so you have more authentic conversations, which are not just about making the sales but also about understanding what will help someone get closer to their goal with you than without you.

There are actions your business can take which will remove the heavy lifting from sales conversations. This includes content, but it's also extended to key marketing actions that require neither a big budget nor compromising your integrity. It's about the actions you can do to simplify sales. In this part of the book, I will cover three simple processes and systems that will create ease when attracting more sales into your business.

Let's start with the first point, repetition. Repetition refers to having clients who come back to you – although it is also tied into repetition of messaging, it's clients we are talking about now. You may have heard it said it is 'cheaper to retain an existing client than acquire a new one'. This highlights that building and maintaining relationships with current customers is generally more cost-effective than the time, effort, and resources required to attract new customers.

Existing customers are more likely to make repeat purchases and refer others to your business, which further reduces marketing costs and boosts profitability. Review clients who have already worked with you previously or search for potential clients who already worked with other coaches, consultants or creatives in a related field. This is not about stealing clients but speaking to those who are already invested in the journey that you support them with.

Let's look at this from a product point of view. Consider a brand like Adidas, which may have a new addition to its collection. Their potential buyer will fall into several criteria. Firstly, they are going to be someone who values investing in trainers. Secondly, they are highly likely to already wear the brand or be influenced by peers who do. Thirdly, it is highly unlikely they will wear Nike or Puma. Both of these are competitor brands that attract the same level of loyalty. The most effective way the Adidas trainers might attract new customers or impact how the brand is perceived would be through a collaboration with another designer (for example, Gucci) and sponsorship or marketing with celebrities or sports personalities. Another relatable example might be the PC versus Apple debate.

I was recently on Facebook and my friend and business pal Leah asked for recommendations for a new laptop that wasn't an Apple. The thread of responses showed the clear camps of those who spoke only the language of Apple and those who didn't. And neither were for turning! Therefore, if Apple were marketing a new addition to their home office portfolio of products, they'd have two very different approaches for those already invested in the brand and those that would need a lot of persuading.

Let's consider how this translates to your customer base. For your higher ticket offers, who is most likely to buy? Someone who has already invested either with you or another coach in a related field? Or someone who has had no exposure to the area you support? For example, if you are a high ticket launch strategist, it is unlikely people who work with you will have had no previous exposure to a business coach in their business. Certainly, for your higher value, high-touch services, what you are looking for is not always someone who has invested with you but who has experience working with a coach at that higher level.

I worked with a client recently who had a brand new programme they wanted to launch, but they did not want to go through a 'loud' social media launch as that felt (in their words) too salesy. They worked in the mental health and well-being area and use their platform predominantly to support and educate, so social selling wasn't their first choice. What they did have, though, was a loyal and engaged community across emails, events and a Facebook group. We looked at who was already in their world and had indicated an interest in the problem being solved. Who had downloaded a free lead magnet, joined their Facebook group, had a conversation in the DMs or joined a previous event?

Instigating a conversation with people who have already shown some engagement increases the likelihood of intent to buy but also the relevance of what you have on offer. By taking this approach to my client's brand-new programme, they could sell out all the places without having one social media promotion. However, before you reach out and make an invitation based on a problem shared in a previous conversation (which may have been some time ago), the first step is to see where they are now and check if what you have on offer will still feel relevant.

A good test for how adept you are at building conversation and community is to look at the DMs or messages you last sent. Are they only ever sales conversations? If they are, you will be coming across as salesy. Build that genuine conversation, get to understand and connect, and you will be better placed to extend relevant offers.

When you consider potential clients who may have invested elsewhere, a good question to ask in the DMs and on sales calls when they share the challenges they face is: What else have you tried or what have you tried that has worked? What you want to identify here is what level of experience, exposure and knowledge they have about the problem you are looking to solve. Particularly with higher ticket offers, it will be rare someone will invest with little to no exposure to the topic you are supporting. Have you a record of every person who has attended a masterclass or downloaded your lead magnet? Do you know who is opening your emails and clicking links? These are your biggest indicators someone sees relevance in what you do.

THE GOLD IS IN THE REPETITION

There is the saying 'new level, new devil', and that is the case for any growth or development. Repetition is also about optimising each stage of the new problem your client experiences. For example, as a fitness coach helping women over forty feel motivated to get to the gym, your first step is most likely going to be building their confidence in the gym and supporting them to understand their why. This might be a 6-month programme of support. However, what do you have in place after the programme has finished? What they will need after six months is very different to their entry point.

Every stage of your dream client's journey will unlock a new problem. Be clear you understand the pain points at every level. You may not want to support at every level, or you may offer programmes for your clients once they 'graduate', but you do not have to publicly market to all of those levels. The point is that a client who has worked with you once is more likely to work with you again than someone unknown to you.

Remember that where they started will not be the same point they will finish after working with you. And as they move along the process, they also may no longer need to just be spoken to about pain points, as I have already shared, but more about their desire and vision for the next level.

Repetition is not just about doing the same thing repeatedly – it's about recognising the value already within your reach. Converting existing clients is not only more cost-effective but also more aligned with the heart-led approach. When you focus on clients who already know, like and trust you, the heavy lifting has already been done.

They've experienced your value, so the path to helping them again is much smoother, requiring less time, energy, and expense than starting afresh. This isn't just a smart business move; it's a way to honour the connections you've built, bringing more heart and less hustle into your sales process. The next way in which you can make sales easier for your business is an all-important one, but can feel incredibly uncomfortable, so let's tackle that now.

CHAPTER 14

THE FORTUNE IS IN THE FOLLOW-UP

'Am I being pushy?' Is that what runs through your mind when you're about to reach back out to someone? It's a common fear – worrying you'll appear pushy, annoying, or desperate. But following up isn't about bothering someone; it's about reminding them of your value, reigniting their interest, and showing you care enough to stay connected. This is especially true when you consider that most people are busy and aren't always proactive (often because they are busy).

Therefore, checking back in and simply asking can be one of the most valuable actions in sales. Following up can feel like the biggest hurdle, yet when you get more comfortable with it, and it is done correctly, it could have the biggest impact on your business. In this chapter we are talking about the number of times a message is repeated and you follow up.

Long before the days of social media, the repetition of a message was seen as increasing the propensity to sales. That all important follow-up. The number of touchpoints required before making a sale has evolved significantly. While it was once thought to be around seven, as I've shared before, we are now looking at over thirty touchpoints before someone purchases. The value in the follow-up is making it easier for those who are ready to step forward and invest by helping them keep it front of mind without crossing the threshold into harassment.

In case that leaves you uncomfortable, think about what would happen if you didn't ask. Probably nothing, you wouldn't hear from them again and they'd likely invest that money elsewhere. Another powerful action is to reframe what it means if someone doesn't respond. The average person sees over 6000 pieces of information a day, receives over 100 emails and is presented with multiple options with most of them. Asking someone if they are still facing a specific issue or if the problem you solve is still relevant to them, is seeking permission to then share what you have on offer. Asking once is also rarely enough. I do feel strongly, though, that you should seek permission before sharing an offer. Let me explain with examples.

Have you ever had a conversation with a dream client on social media, met in person at an event, engaged during a free masterclass or even had a sales call and then, later, had a relevant offer? You would naturally want to reach back out. One of the best ways is to ask how they are getting on with the problem they have previously shared. In doing this, you are personalising your DM or email, reminding them of a challenge, and checking in. If they still face that challenge, or have the same goal, you can 'seek permission' to share something relevant you are working on now.

You make it easier for someone to step forward if now is the right time for them. Two check-ins are not harassment if you have built a relationship, so long as the only time you connect isn't just to sell. You also need to nurture your audience and build genuine relationships.

Consider the other ways you are making your audience aware of what is available. Where else are you repeating the message around your offer that will contribute to the thirty plus touchpoints the average person needs before they invest? Your social media posts, emails, updating bios, etc? On average, only ten per cent of your audience see your content. So why wouldn't you repeat your message and make it easier to step forward?

One way to make it easier to know who you are speaking to, what they have shared, or when you last had an engagement is to track this. I am talking about a good old spreadsheet, which is your customer relationship management system (CRM). CRM systems have always been crucial during my sales career, as they keep you on top of conversations and potential customers. You can invest in systems that do this, although a simple spreadsheet can suffice, depending on the scale of how many people you engage and speak to. Whatever you use, it will only be as good as the information you add.

To ensure you are GDPR compliant, be alert to how you are storing sensitive information. GDPR refers to the storing of personal, identifiable data online. The same is true of what you might copy and paste into an AI tool like ChatGPT. If you are unsure of the guidelines, read up on them online. Another tip with your potential dream clients and client notes is to make them factual, and a good rule of thumb is to ask yourself if you would be comfortable with your client reading what you have written. And, finally, password-protect files if they contain identifiable data.

Once you have clear data on your leads, it will be easier to follow them up. I have seen with my own and many clients' businesses the number of times people will buy after they have been personally contacted about a relevant offer despite believing you have already shared the offer 'everywhere'. They most likely didn't see your social media post, take in your Instagram story, or saw it and forgot about it even when it was of interest. I understand it can feel uncomfortable to follow up with someone who hasn't responded. After all, ego comes into play, and not following up also protects you from feelings of 'rejection'. The truth is no one pays as much attention as you think.

The likelihood is you are reaching out to people already connected to you, following your content, and opting into your emails, so the reframe is making it easier for them to find what they need and help them decide. How often should you follow up? That depends on the existing relationship. But as I shared earlier, as a rule of thumb, if you can see more than two messages in a row in their DMs, un-seen or unanswered, consider how else you can be front of mind and nurture the relationship. Sometimes, it isn't the time, and you are not the priority. If this is the case, make a note and keep engaged with their content and keep that genuine connection, regardless of whether they choose to come back to you.

But what about when someone does respond, but the answer is a 'no' or a 'not right now'? It's easy to take that personally, to let it deflate your enthusiasm or even cause you to doubt your offering. However, a 'no' isn't the end of the conversation; it's a pause. It's an opportunity to strengthen the relationship and continue nurturing that connection without expectations. If your potential client is still in communication, it enables you to know more about why now is not the time.

I ran a workshop recently and considered who would be a good match. I emailed people personally before my group email to my subscribers went out. On the day my emails went out, no one responded. Yet they were all known to me, had worked with me, and we had a great rapport. It would have been so easy to assume they were not interested. A few days later, I had a couple of polite responses thanking me for my invitation but sharing why it was not suitable at this time. That still left at least a handful of people I had not heard back from. So, I sent a second email. I had a few more responses, and a few people signed up. It still left a few more people known to me who did not reply.

My mind could have convinced me I was being rejected. Fortunately, I've learnt not to always listen to my mind and remember my objective is just to make it easier for people to step forward where and when it feels like my solution is a fit for their problem. So, I took to my Instagram stories and posted an invitation to the workshop, asking my audience to vote if they would like more information. Several people who had received my personalised email voted in my Instagram stories that they wanted to know more. I stepped into the DMs to discuss it further, and they were ready to book. When I asked if they had seen my email, Michelle told me she had, but hadn't realised it was personalised and wanted to proceed. Another, Lauren, said she had but had got caught up and forgot to reply, and Nicola shared it was just what she needed and didn't recall an email. Imagine if I had not followed up?

So, when you think about follow-up, consider it as a

continuation of the conversation – a way to show you're invested in the success and prospects of clients. It's not just about making a sale, but building relationships for transformative results. Following up isn't a task to check off your list; it's a commitment to the people you want to serve. And that's where the real fortune lies.

CHAPTER 15

THE VALUE IS IN THE AUTHENTIC SALES VOICE

What is authenticity in sales, and can the two go hand in hand? As we come to the final chapter of the book, I hope you will see they most definitely can. With time, you will develop a style of selling that feels aligned with who you are and who you want to attract, and, as is very much the case in the coaching world, who you are becoming.

One of the most common areas of discomfort around sales is feeling it is scripted, especially for heart-led business owners who may not feel this is aligned with their values or even what they teach. But as we have spoken about in detail, mastery in sales revolves around connection, understanding what your dream client wants, and the symptoms of not having this. Whilst I have shared a roadmap with you for conversations and guidelines for the foundation of sales, there is a reason why I did not share scripts. Because I see that as an important guide but not a one-size-fits-all. You must find a style that works for you whilst being aware of the logic and psychology around how the questions are asked and the order to ask them. Speaking in someone else's words during a sales call and through your content will become evident.

If your dream clients do not feel a connection or a sense of trust, they will not buy. People buy trust and clarity. They also want to know they will be closer to their goal with you and that the cost of inaction is greater. Developing the style that works best for you is what I have termed your 'authentic sales voice'. How do you know you have your authentic sales voice? You'll feel it, you'll have higher conversion rates, and be working with more clients who get results.

How often have you had the opportunity to buy from one of two people or places and gone with the more expensive option because of the connection you had with the person or company and a greater level of trust? That may come down to many factors, including reputation, but it will also be because of their authentic sales voice. Intuition plays a large part in sales, and taking a step back to look at your business, who you are working with, and their results will help you understand your authentic sales voice.

When clients start working on their business, I often find

that even though they were uncomfortable with it they have worked with scripts. Using scripts is understandable as there is a lot to remember, but I like to think of the sales call as a journey. A roadmap. You know the final destination (to decide along with your potential client on their next steps) and, therefore, the general direction you are going in. Once you are clear on this, as we covered in the chapter on sales conversations, you won't need your script. As with any journey you do multiple times, the route becomes familiar. Sometimes, you will face initial roadblocks and need to detour. Getting comfortable with sales calls, including ones that don't go to plan, is a part of the process.

My career in sales started out working in a heavy target-driven environment, and whilst I enjoyed making money, it wasn't money that was the number one factor that motivated me. It was helping people. And helping people has carried me through my thirty-plus-year career. Being good at sales came from my ability to connect. What's great to see is how much more widely spoken about a more authentic approach to sales is. I've done Instagram and LinkedIn Lives, spoken as an expert on stages, guested on podcasts and been interviewed on YouTube channels with leading sales coaches from across the globe. All of them wanted to discuss this approach further, and there is an army of men and women passionate about teaching this more authentic approach to sales. Your authentic sales voice works best alongside understanding the foundations of human psychology, even at its most basic level.

You may have heard of Maslow's Hierarchy of Needs, which outlines the five levels of human need, and it includes the need to belong, feel safe and feel validated. This is no different in sales; people need to feel heard and seen. This transpires in content that shows your dream clients you know them and how they are feeling and also on sales calls where the purpose isn't for them to learn more about you but for you to learn more about what they need.

I recall working with a coach who wanted to grow the sales of her business. Her work was deeply ethical, and understandably, she had resistance to sales scripts for fear of sounding wooden and inauthentic. Whilst scripts can feel unnatural, I showed her how to use prompts, or a roadmap as I have called it. Once you understand the purpose of the questions, you no longer need a script in front of you, but it is there to help you understand why you ask the questions you ask, the purpose of the call and how it supports your dream client. Once you can visualise the roadmap – that's the journey your questions need to take your dream clients on, the questions you ask will feel logical, and you will be able to guide sales conversations with ease.

This is when you get to develop your most authentic voice. Whether a sales call or a DM on social media, be clear about the intention of the conversation and what it is you need to know about them. Be genuinely curious, listen and remember that you may be the tenth person trying to 'sell to them' that day. Setting aside time in your working day to have conversations with potential leads not only gets easier but is also a core part of your role. Very few have the luxury of sitting back and waiting for business to come in. When you come from a place of genuine curiosity and a desire to help, I promise you it won't feel salesy.

How do you identify your authentic sales voice? It starts with sounding like you. But if that's all you do, you'll miss the sales part. Hiding behind a chat and a cup of tea as a sales call is doing a disservice to potential clients. Get comfortable in the fact sales are business and receiving money for your service is an exchange for the transformation you offer. Once you have those foundations and begin to understand the journey a sales conversation is designed to take a client on, you get to think about building this with your authentic voice. This personalisation creates a deeper connection in your content and conversations.

Without context, I'm not likely to answer a DM from someone I don't know trying to send me a salesy unsolicited message. Equally, being asked by a stranger in my LinkedIn DMs after we've connected what flavour of crisps I like (yes, really) seems a little pointless, too. Finding your authentic voice is as much about being clear on the intention of the conversation. If people feel suspicious when you contact them, or feel like they are being sold to, you will once again be back in the land of sales 'ick'.

I've touched on the value of data, and I would encourage you to look at yours. Task yourself with several conversations in a week including connection conversations in the DMs. This could simply be an extension of a comment under your content, new follower conversations and clarity calls. I'm not going to tell you how many of these to have, but these are core sales-generating activities, and you should be prioritising time to do this every day in your business. Tracking the data shows how effective these conversations are for you. Start each conversation from a place of curiosity of whether they need something you may be able to help with. If you're sending one DM a day and having one clarity call a week, having a 100% success rate and making enough sales to sustain your business, you have your answer.

The results you want will determine your output and where you need to focus or refine the conversation. A lot of people are put off by the term data; if that's you, call it something else! In essence, it is a record that will help you build your future pipeline, see what people have said, how interested they are and how they have responded to how you can help. This information helps you cultivate your authentic sales voice so consider the data as simply a self-reflection in a spreadsheet. Listening is one of the most powerful tools you can cultivate in sales success and helps lead the conversation where it feels most natural whilst understanding the purpose of the conversation. The data you collect is simply feedback for yourself so you can refine and look for the best tools for growth.

One pitfall of so much content online is that you can inadvertently fall into the trap of replicating someone else's sales voice and style. Whilst few ideas are original, trying to be someone else through your sales content and conversations will be obvious. When you attempt to adopt methods and styles that don't align with your personality or values, this will become misaligned with your purpose. I've lost count of screenshots shared with me of two identical pieces of content. It's most often a sign that the person mimicking has not developed confidence in their authentic sales voice. How many times have you met someone whose offline presence differs greatly from how they show up online? That's where your authentic sales voice comes in, from the words you use, the visuals, and how distinct your purpose, values, vision, mission and promise are. Whilst those are part of your brand values, they are all key in building the foundations of your authentic sales voice.

Your authentic sales voice also means getting clear on what you cannot do but also having the confidence to be clear on what you do. Many entrepreneurs have told me they have dimmed their voice because of one bad client experience, or because they aren't running an award-winning podcast or business. They feel like an imposter. I love to use the example of one of the most successful football managers in the world,

Sir Alex Ferguson, who was known for being a world-class manager despite not being a world-class footballer. Yet the two were possible.

Your authentic sales voice is also deeply connected to your self-belief, and the two need to be worked on hand in hand. The more confidence your dream clients see in you, the more confident they will be that you have the tools to get them closer to their goals. Your authentic sales voice is also about being sure who you are not for and who you cannot help.

As we've spoken about, what makes you unique is you. Another part of your authentic sales voice will be your specific take, such as your methodology and uniquely coined phrases. People also respond well to real, relatable experiences and connections; just be careful to get the balance right, as sales conversations and calls and even your content must leave your dream clients feeling like you know them, not just that they know you. When you talk about yourself, it should show how that helps them.

There is no business without sales, and in this book, we have focused on the how. There are pages and guides you can mark, and even examples of how to navigate sales conversations in the DMs through to sales calls themselves. As I shared at the beginning, the 'how' is super important, but the 'why' is the linchpin. Because without your why, the how won't work. And your why, especially as a coach, creative or visionary, will help you understand your dream client's why. It starts with curious conversations and building your authentic sales voice, so sales become an effortless part of your business.

TASK 5: MAP OUT YOUR SALES-GENERATING WEEK

This final task is about planning your week with intention by focusing on the key sales activities that will grow your business. It's about setting yourself up for success by ensuring your diary is filled with actions that matter such as sending DMs, following up, and booking clarity calls. Here's how to do it:

1. Consider what you have learnt so far and identify the following:

Three essential sales-generating activities to focus on each week. These are activities whose sole function is to directly help you attract, connect, converse with and possibly convert more of your dream clients. This could include:

- Sending a set number of DMs to potential clients or reconnecting with leads.
- Following up with people you've spoken to but haven't converted.
- Booking in and running clarity calls.

- Sending an email to your audience with an offer.

2. Block Out Time in Your Diary

Next decide when you're going to work on these activities and block specific time slots in your diary. Keep it simple, such as:

- 30 minutes a day for sending DMs.
- 1 hour twice a week for following up with leads.
- 2 hours for discovery calls or consultations.

Diarise these blocks of time as you would a client call. I recommend to do this earlier in your day rather than push it to the end. The idea is for this to feel like a key part of your business day.

3. Review and Adjust

At the end of each week, review what worked and what didn't. Adjust your diary for the next week, making sure you're focused on the actions that are most effective for you. This might be a weekly tracker where you can track your progress or, perhaps, a pipeline where you record everything from who you have engaged with on social media through to your leads and future pipeline.

AND FINALLY...

Most sales books finish with a promise that you now know everything you need about sales. I'm not going to do that. The truth is that learning never ends. As a coach, creative, or entrepreneur, you'll keep evolving and so will your sales style. I've worked in sales for over thirty years, and I'm not the same salesperson I was last year, let alone five years ago. Whilst the fundamentals of sales remain the same, growth is constant, and that's the exciting part.

Instead of seeing this book as the end, treat it as your foundation. Think of it as my gift, the foundation of sales coaching in a book, minus the high-ticket coaching price tag. Building a business takes time. That's why so many people start with referrals and these don't happen overnight. It takes time to build your reputation, grow your network, and establish yourself with a new audience. The commitment to learning isn't just about knowledge, studying or even personal growth, but applying what you learn.

By now, I hope you feel more confident about sales. More than anything, I want this book to change how you see sales, sparking curiosity and even a desire to get good at it. How you think about sales matters. Your mindset around it influences how you show up, your conversations and, ultimately, the results you see.

I've seen so many social media posts and comments from people saying that sales make them uncomfortable or 'icky'. I see questions on forums from business owners asking how to grow their business without selling.

You can't. There's no way to grow or even sustain a business without cash in the bank. But what I have shown you is that sales aren't some separate task you 'have' to do – it's a natural part of your business. It's about having real conversations, getting curious and finding your authentic sales voice.

This isn't the end of your learning; it's just the beginning. It's ever-evolving, just like you and your business. Be open and expect change. You'll grow and shift, and so should the foundations of your business. No matter how long you've been in business, it's never too late to revisit the basics. Sometimes, it's essential.

You'll hear a lot of promises about overnight success, but the reality is that building a sustainable business takes time and effort. It's not easy, no matter what anyone tells you. And that's okay. True success is built from the ground up, layer by layer, brick by brick. The truth is that overnight success – when it does happen – is rarely sustainable.

This is the book you should read before, or even while, getting coached. It's the guide to revisit when you're lost or unsure. It's your reminder that the foundations are where everything starts.

THE VALUE IS IN THE AUTHENTIC SALES VOICE

You don't need to have it all figured out. You just need to start. Let go of perfectionism and fall in love with what sales makes possible – not just for your business but for the people you're here to serve. Because when you get sales right, you're not just changing your life, you're changing theirs too.

That's what this heart-led sales journey is really about.

HOW TO STAY IN TOUCH

Below are several ways to keep this conversation going or connect with me. There is also a bonus chapter for those who want to learn more about heart-led sales.

SOCIAL MEDIA:
instagram.com/iamsumanrandhawa
linkedin.com/in/iamsumanrandhawa

WEBSITE:
sumanrandhawa.com

EMAIL:
info@sumanrandhawa.com

BONUS CHAPTER:
Access my Curious Conversations Framework for more on how to have effortless conversations in the DMs, and you can opt-in to keep in touch for more sales tips and insights.

academy.luxuryofbusiness.com/conversation-framework

ACKNOWLEDGEMENTS

No book is complete without acknowledgements. Writing a book for me might have been a bit like mastering sales for you. It's been a labour of love trying to find time to write whilst running a business, growing my brand, and being a human being! I couldn't have done it without the support and encouragement of my loved ones, friends, coaches and clients. I won't possibly be able to list everyone, but I want to make some specific mentions.

The key to this whole book is my book coach, Amy Warren, who patiently worked with me from the start with many a morning keeping me accountable at 7 a.m. for writing sprints, even though I declared 'I don't do 7 a.m. starts', for supporting and encouraging me and the hours you've spent on my manuscript. All I can say is it's amazing what you can do when you try. I now do 7 a.m. starts and write books… I wanted this book to show you what is possible for us all, and that includes for your small business and sales.

Also, a special mention to my two nephews, Rien and Reece Sandhu, for being my number one fans and asking me regularly about the book and my entrepreneurial journey. I hope you're as proud of me as I am of you. I'm just sorry I couldn't fulfil your request for a picture of you both in the book!

Specific thanks are also extended to those who have been instrumental throughout the last few years of building my business: Victoria Abascal, Anirudh Agarwal, Caoimhe Harrison, Leah Gregory, Suzy Ashworth, Yinka Ewuola, Richard Moore, Julian McKenzie, Andrew Pickering, Pete Gartland, Krish Surroy, Priya Sandhu, Ricky Sandhu and, of course, my mum. You've all been a huge support, and each taught me something valuable. Thank you for your unwavering belief and support.

ABOUT THE AUTHOR

Suman Randhawa is an award-winning mentor, consultant and keynote speaker dedicated to helping online coaches and creatives ignite heart-led sales and build more powerful connections.

With over three decades of experience in senior commercial sales roles, she has worked for major media sales teams and as part of the senior management team for the leading luxury brand, Harrods.

Through Suman's career, she has learned the power of aligning sales with heart and purpose, while repositioning 'failure' as the biggest source of growth.

Suman launched her business days before her 50th birthday, transforming lifelong skills into more than just transactional knowledge. She now teaches solopreneurs how to thrive through genuine connection and meaningful impact. Her mission is simple: to debunk outdated sales stereotypes and prove that sales can be ethical and empowering, and are essential for business success.

Featured on radio and global podcasts, and standing on stages alongside figures like Davina McCall, Suman has built a distinct voice in amplifying sales for coaches and creatives. In 2024, she was honoured to receive the Businesswoman of the Year award.